Object-Oriented Programming:

A New Way of Thinking

Object-Oriented Programming:

A New Way of Thinking

by

Donald W. and Lori A. MacVittie

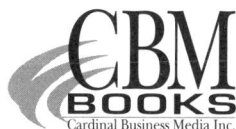

CBM BOOKS
Cardinal Business Media Inc.

Trademark Acknowledgments

Library of Congress Cataloging-in-Publication Data

MacVittie, Donald, 1966-

The handy oo book : exploring object-oriented technology / by Donald W. and Lori A. MacVittie.
p. cm.
Includes bibliographical references and index.
     ISBN 1-878956-52-3
     1. Object-oriented programming (Computer science)
     I. MacVittie, Lori A., 1969-
     II. Title.
     QA76.64.M32 1995
     005.13--dc20   95-23307
                        CIP

Please address comments and questions to the publisher:

CBM Books
1300 Virginia Drive, Suite #400
Fort Washington, PA 19034
(215) 643-8000 FAX (215) 643-8099

Editor: Andrea Zavod
Production Manager: Laura Derr
Typesetting: Richard Lowden

Dedication

*To our parents, for their encouragement
to follow our dreams, their support,
and the work ethic they lovingly forced upon us.*

*To Korey, for his understanding
when mom and dad were
too busy writing to play. We love you.*

*To the memory of Dr. Der Jei Lin,
whose constant attempt to challenge
every pupil made not only better students,
but better people
- Don.*

*To Dr. Bruce Mielke, whose attempts
to convince me that calculus was fun failed,
but whose challenges to learn more
and follow tangents worked like a charm
- Lori.*

Table of Contents

Part Two
Analysis and Design of
Object-Oriented Systems 87

Table of Figures

Table of Listings

Who Should Read This Book

We wrote the *Handy OO Book* with experienced structured programmers and systems managers in mind. The purpose of the book is to explore the necessary change in the way developers think, and in the department's operation, in order to move into the object-oriented (OO) world.

If you have read any one of the several books available on object-oriented programming (OOP) or object-oriented design (OOD), you know that there is a ton of (often confusing) terminology involved in object-oriented development, as well as page after page of notations and, often times, strange mathematical figures.

In addition to this, there seems to be something missing from the methodologies. That something is the thought processes needed to become an object-oriented developer. It is that something that explains just exactly how an object developer's view of the world is different from that of a structured programmer. Here, we have attempted to address those thought processes and views, and tried to sort out all of the information available about object-oriented systems development, and present it in a clear and concise manner suitable for structured programmers to digest.

In this book, you will not find a lot of information about language syntax, rave object-oriented analysis and design methodologies, or the advantages of a given language over another (this book contains some comparison of languages, however). What you will find instead is a guide to how to think in an object-oriented manner.

We have also added some tips about managing object developers. Many of them make sense in the structured world, but because of the complexity of problems usually solved with object-oriented code, they become almost imperative when managing an object-oriented team.

The object paradigm is a realm full of fun and impressive terms, many of which will be foreign to you. In order to help your voyage into this new technology, we have also included a glossary of the most common, and some uncommon, object-oriented terms.

Why Move to OO?

It seems that the whole world is moving toward object-oriented technology. It is considered cutting-edge technology without which your company will be left in the dark ages. While this is certainly not true, there are some definite advantages to moving into the object-oriented arena. There is a plethora of development tools and libraries available for the technology, which gives developers a wider array of choices during the development process.

In addition, the code written by developers, if done correctly, can be made into reusable components. This can reduce development time of future endeavors. If your enterprise is modeled correctly, new applications can be built upon those components in a relatively short period of time, because there is no need to re-engineer those components in order to fit them into a new and different project. Productivity can be increased, making it possible to complete more projects on time and more quickly—making your company more profitable and productive.

Object-oriented technology also makes sense. It more closely models the real world and therefore allows your system to act in a manner that is consistent with the way your business works. It is also easier to build a system that contains components that can be mapped directly to your business. Imagine discussing your system with a non-programmer. The user must understand functions, procedures and variables in order to understand what your system is doing. When we discuss object-oriented systems with users, we can talk in terms that are understandable from both a business and a software point of view. 'A customer does this, that and the other thing' is more understandable by a user than, 'This function changes x, y or z about a customer.' The protocol for discussions about requirements changes and permits not only the user to understand the system being created, but allows the developer to understand the business better—something that in the long run can only make the system better.

Introduction

If you are a structured programmer, there are two things you must do before exploring this paradigm any further :

1. Forget everything you know about structured programming.
2. Forget some more.

There are several languages that support object-oriented programming. Examples in this book will be done in Borland International's C++ (conforming to the ANSI Standard, or what might eventually be the standard someday), Borland International's Turbo Pascal with Objects, and Digitalk's Smalltalk/V.

We chose these particular languages for several reasons. C++ builds on the syntax of C, which is a popular PC language in business operations today and therefore has a large base of programmers. Smalltalk is growing as a viable pure object-oriented solution for many businesses and was included for its purity in the paradigm. Pascal was included for two reasons: it is similar to many other languages, and it is perhaps the easiest to learn. With the advent of Borland International's newest development tool, Delphi, Pascal may make its way into the businesses realm in the near future.

This book does not attempt to teach you to program in any of the languages, but rather to give you an overview of them. Its focus is mainly on object-oriented principles, ideas, techniques and thought processes, in addition to the analysis and design of object systems. This book was designed for managers and those who have not yet entered the object-oriented paradigm, but who are considering doing so. The content should aid in the decision making process of jumping into object land, but also will provide a preliminary glance of three of today's most prevalent object-oriented languages.

Part One

The Object-Oriented Paradigm : An Overview

CHAPTER 1
The Object-Oriented Paradigm

"Object types are the fundamental difference between object-oriented languages and traditional procedural languages" (Entsminger 1990 42). While this is an interesting perspective, it is not altogether true. While objects are implemented as *types* in extended traditional procedural languages, within the paradigm they are not truly types. In addition, the fundamental differences between traditional structured programming and object-oriented programming (OOP) go far deeper than just the use of objects. The object-oriented paradigm is not so much a programming technique as it is a way of thinking.

"Object-oriented programming ... is a new way of thinking about problem solving with computers. Instead of trying to mold the problem into something familiar to the computer, the object-oriented approach adapts the computer to the problem" (Eckel 1993, 3).

Object-oriented programming attempts to model, or map, real-world entities into similar entities in the computer spectrum. A structured model is always discussed in terms of functions, and what those functions are doing to data, instead of the other way around. Design, in the structured paradigm, involves creating new functions that take in structures and variables and act upon them. A typical insertion into some sort of list demands that the list and new data are both passed to a function that will manipulate the list and add the new data to it. In the object realm, you would simply tell the list to insert a new object (new data) into itself. Structured programming does not map to the real world consistently, or logically.

You *can* do so in an object-oriented environment. Structured programmers see things as modules, functions and structures. It is a matter of what has to be done, and what data is needed to get it done. Object-oriented programmers think in terms of objects and messages in a way that says what information do I need and how does it need to act? They are almost at completely opposite ends of a spectrum, one data centric, one function specific.

The problem with structured techniques is that it does not closely resemble the real world, in fact, we must alter the real world in order to make it fit into the tightly defined world of structured programming.

In the real world, a cat chases a mouse and a dog chases a cat. The animal has a specific associated behavior, which may be common to its entire family. Their behaviors are specific to the animal, in that particular attributes of the animal are used in those behaviors. Cats and dogs communicate through the manipulation of their voices, but crickets communicate by manipulating their back legs.

We frequently think in terms of an object (a person, an animal, etc.) having attributes and behaviors. When we sit down to design an application we should carry this perspective, and not abandon it in favor of a methodology that forces us to change our view of the real world in order to fit it into our tightly knit, structured computerized world. And, if we practice this way of thinking, we can make our time coding much more efficient, simpler and easier to re-use.

A kitten is a feline, but so is a tiger. A data structure defining these would contain many of the same attributes, and some different. The object-oriented paradigm allows us to define a feline that has attributes specific to both kittens and tigers (and any other feline for that matter), and later create specific instances of that data structure that allow us to add attributes that are specific to a kitten or tiger. You write the common code one time, and from then on you don't need to not write it again, unless you are changing some basic attribute or behavior. Isn't that the way we describe these things in our own lives? We describe things in terms of is_a hierarchies, that things are like a certain other thing except for a couple of specific attributes or actions, etc. For example, puppy is a dog is a canine is a mammal.

We are fundamentally object-oriented in our daily lives. It only makes sense to use that which is inherent in us to make our software definition process simple, without losing quality or the ability to closely replicate the complexity that the end user has come to expect.

Object-oriented techniques are used in many different areas, some of which are not even related to application development. Douglas R. Hofstadter uses the object-oriented paradigm to discuss human communication theory, and expert-systems design uses object-oriented concepts in designing inference engines. Semantic networks are based on a concept called *frames*, which are, on a basic level, objects.

Many other fields have benefited from this point of view, and finally application development has begun to reap the benefits of the object-oriented paradigm. The concept of object orientation has been around for a long time, it is only recently that it was given a name and has thus grown into a true paradigm. Exploiting the natural intuitiveness of object-oriented concepts gives this paradigm an edge in the realm of computer science.

What is an Object?

We often speak of this object entity as if it were corporeal, as if it had a life of its own. A software object closely resembles a real-world object. It represents some tangible entity and has attributes that distinguish it from other objects in the system. It has behaviors that represent its real world counterparts' behaviors.

For example, if we have modeled a customer object after a real customer, the object might have behaviors such as placeOrder, cancelOrder, or makePayment . It also has attributes that are an integral part of the object, usually corresponding to some attribute of the real world entity.

If we again examine our customer object, it might have such attributes as name, number and address. A customer can be an object, and so can a business, an employee, and even a process. A software object exists as an entity with attributes and is capable of sending and responding to messages. Objects interact with one another in order to complete a task necessary to the business processes of the system.

When a developer writes code and creates a class, he is creating a template for some object. This template defines the attributes of the object and the way in which the object will interact with other objects in the system. When the application is running and an instance of that class is created, you have instantiated an object.

There is a definite difference between the class and the instance of a class. When you create a class, you are saying that everything of this type will have these abilities and these attributes. For example, when defining a person, every person will have a name, hair color, eye color, and an intelligence quotient. Every person will be able to communicate, eat and drink. When a real person is born they have been, in a way, created. It works the same with a software object. The basic attributes and abilities are defined, and when the program actually says 'create a new X or Y,' a new object is born. We call this an instance of X or Y, or an object of type X or Y.

With this in mind, a developer might sit down and write the definition of a customer, taking the attributes and abilities of an actual customer and using it to define the template from which customer objects will be created. The customer might have a name, a unique number, an address and a phone number. The customer's abilities would depend on the type of business in which they are involved. At a bank, for example, these abilities might include those of making transactions with the bank or with other entities.

This is essentially the concept of an object—a group of data items and protocols that closely resemble the real world and drive the application. An object can be as meaningful or as abstract as the developer wishes—it all depends on the application being built and the needs of the company.

Requirements of a Language

There are four basic attributes required in order for a language to be considered object-oriented :

- Data Encapsulation
- Data Abstraction
- Inheritance
- Polymorphism

Several languages support the object-oriented paradigm— C++ and Borland's Turbo Pascal with Objects are both popular and used frequently in both academia and in the real world. Smalltalk is known as a pure OO language, because all user defined types are classes, and all processing is done through the use of messages sent to the product of those classes: objects.

Which language is best is a debate best left to those who want to worry about it. Each language is suited to different environments, and even then can be specific to a particular project. Object technology and real-time systems is a growing trend at this time, but in most cases, a complex C++ or Smalltalk system would not be the first choice for a real-time system. This is because of the nature of the language and its implementation more than because of the technology. Which one is best suited to your current project is your decision.

For a language to qualify as object-oriented it must meet these four requirements. Some languages are inherently object-oriented, such as Lisp, and others have been modified to support OO, such as COBOL and OPS5 (OOPS5 is the object-oriented version). ADA 95 also supports object-oriented programming. Eiffel is another pure object-oriented language, one of few that also supports multiple inheritance. C and Pascal have been used as a base language upon which their object-oriented counterparts have been built.

Some languages, such as C, can be forced to simulate the object paradigm, but lack some important facet of an object-oriented language: including inheritance, C structures can contain functions—simulating and encapsulation methods, and limit access to its data fields through the use of these methods—simulating encapsulation. By making structures members of other structures, you can closely simulate abstraction, but there is no way to support inheritance.

An OOP language must support all of the four attributes, but up until implementation time the language is less relevant than it is with a procedural language. It is the concepts and methodologies behind the object-oriented paradigm that give it its power, not necessarily the language.

Data Encapsulation

Data encapsulation is the process of localizing data definition, hiding data within an object, and allowing access to it only through special functions known as *member func-*

tions, methods or *messages*. Which term you prefer or use depends heavily on the language in which you develop. We will use the term *method* in order to remain consistent.

Methods define the operations that occur on a given piece or set of *data members*, such as setting and retrieving their value. They are often also referred to as manipulation methods, because they manipulate the data unlike accessor methods, which simply set or retrieve values. The data within an object is not, or should not be, accessed directly by other entities. The methods defined are directly related to the data, and affect some pieces of data within the object.

Data encapsulation is used as a security tool, as an error handler, and for data validation. Perhaps the data is an encrypted password, and the methods you define decrypt and encrypt that password. You do not want other classes accessing the data member directly. The possibility of corrupting the data increases with the number of external classes directly accessing the data.

Encapsulation helps to prevent this. Data validation and error checking, when handled by the class, reduces the need for other classes to do the same extensive checking when processing data it receives from another class. Encapsulation is also a good tool for managing complexity within large systems.

Because encapsulation means that the data is hidden, there are many choices of what data type to choose for any given data member. Some data members become more references, as in the index of a book. They are more like 'see XXX' data members than actual objects. It sometimes makes sense to simply store some significant piece of another object's data than the object itself. Some of these situations are more obvious than others, and it is those subtle situations that we will discuss in *Chapter 8*.

Data Abstraction

Data abstraction is the process of grouping together attributes and actions specifically related to a single entity. Common attributes and responsibilities are grouped together to form a logical unit called a *class*. The sum of the attributes makes up the whole.

For example, when speaking to a person on the phone you do not have to know his hair color, eye color, height or weight in order to know the person to whom you are speaking. These aspects of the entity are pieces of the whole which are not necessarily important in all instances, but that are important to the overall definition of the entity. You don't see the pieces, but the whole, as you do with a person and his features. You may examine features closely, but it is the sum of those features that make the person a unique individual.

A person has attributes that are not specific to any given individual. Therefore, an abstraction of a person would store those basic attributes along with methods to manipulate those attributes (*Figure 1.1*).

```
┌─────────────────────────┐
│ PERSON                  │
├─────────────────────────┤
│ hairColor               │
│ eyeColor                │
│ height                  │
│ weight                  │
│ name                    │
│ gender                  │
└─────────────────────────┘
```

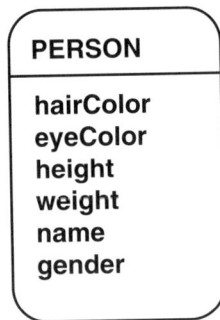

Figure 1.1 : Class Person.

The class is a PERSON, and it has the attributes shown in *Figure 1.1*. The attributes are the most basic features of a person. Other attributes may be job, title, children, spouse, etc., but these are not specific to all people, just to certain people.

This abstraction is simple enough to support all people, and can be used to describe all types of people. The most efficient thing about this system is: once you have written the basic abstract data type (ADT) , you need never write it again (if it was properly abstracted in the first place).

Most basic ADTs (stacks, queues, lists, etc.) can be and have been implemented as generic container classes and except for the purposes of learning the paradigm, it is more efficient to simply find one and use it. Some call this plug-and-play programming, others simply call it the best thing to hit programming since transistors.

Inheritance

We now have a PERSON, but what can we do with it? It is general enough to represent the base of all types of people, but not specific enough to really be of any use to us. Tax companies need a social security number, insurance companies need an ID number, employers need titles and salaries, and so on. Through *inheritance*, you can create a more specific type of person that is suited directly to the needs of the developer.

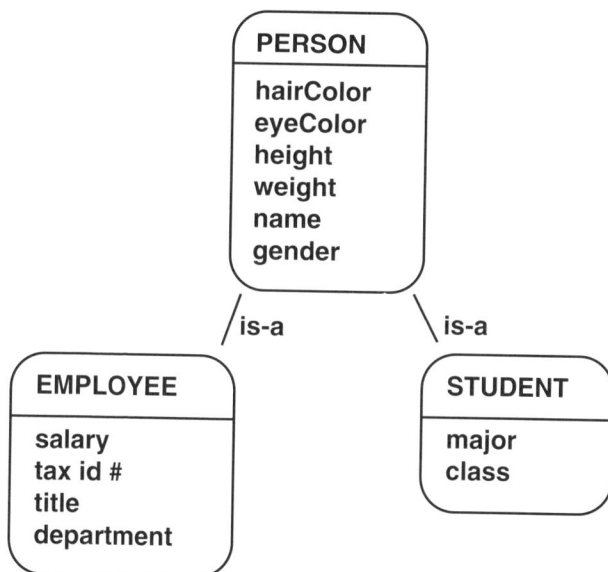

```
              ┌─────────────┐
              │ PERSON      │
              ├─────────────┤
              │ hairColor   │
              │ eyeColor    │
              │ height      │
              │ weight      │
              │ name        │
              │ gender      │
              └─────────────┘
             /is-a      \is-a
┌─────────────┐        ┌─────────────┐
│ EMPLOYEE    │        │ STUDENT     │
├─────────────┤        ├─────────────┤
│ salary      │        │ major       │
│ tax id #    │        │ class       │
│ title       │        └─────────────┘
│ department  │
└─────────────┘
```

Figure 1.2 : A Simple Hierarchy.

In *Figure 1.2* you see that an EMPLOYEE is_a PERSON, containing all the attributes of a person, but also containing attributes that are specific to an employee. Inheritance is often described in terms of is_a hierarchies. A puppy is_a dog, a dog is_a mammal, a mammal is_a warm-blooded animal. This approach mirrors our view of the world, and makes our understanding of inheritance and hierarchies a much simpler process.

A STUDENT is also a PERSON, but contains attributes specific to a student, and is very different than an employee. Through inheritance, both STUDENT and EMPLOYEE have access to and will use the attributes of a PERSON in addition to their own specific attributes and methods. But the code written to define and manipulate a PERSON is the same for both STUDENT and EMPLOYEE.

STUDENT and EMPLOYEE are called subclasses of PERSON, or derivations of PERSON. PERSON is known as a base class, because it is the base for STUDENT and EMPLOYEE, and these classes are said to be *derived* from it. STUDENT and EMPLOYEE are also called children or subclasses of PERSON, and PERSON is often referred to as the parent or *super class* of STUDENT and EMPLOYEE.

Polymorphism

Using the idea of inheritance, we can employ the last attribute of an object-oriented language, —*polymorphism* to simplify our manipulations of these abstract data types. In structured languages, a list (array, queue, stack, etc.) can contain only one data type.

In an OOP language you can mix and match different objects in the same list, as long as they are ultimately derived from the same object. Polymorphism allows us to do this. Polymorphism also allows us to engage in processing without requiring us to know the exact type of the data with which we are working. We might have a list of animals, and the processing that we wish to do is to iterate over that list and ask each animal to 'speak.' This might simply entail printing out the animal's particular voice on the screen, such as 'meow,' or 'woof.' If we have defined a class with the behavior of speaking , and then created classes from that class, then all of them will have the same behavior by virtue of inheritance. However, each animal speaks in a different way, so each animal must define it's speaking behavior so that it is correct for the individual animal. If we were to assume that the classes involved were animal at the top level, and cat, dog, and bird at the subclass levels, and further that the behavior was called speak, we could iterate over a list of these animals and tell each one to speak. We would not need to know what specific animal class resides at any given element, because they all have a common protocol, the same behavior.

We can use this to enforce a common protocol across objects and allow such general processing to occur. Let's examine this more closely:

```
Animal—>    speak
            *Cat—>speak "print meow"
            *Dog—>speak "print woof"
            *Bird—>speak "print tweet"
```

If our list is as follows:

```
LIST= Bird - Dog - Cat - Dog - Bird - Bird
```

Then if we iterate over LIST and tell each element to 'speak,' we would see the following

```
tweet    woof    meow    woof    tweet    tweet
```

15

This is the general concept of polymorphism. Using this concept we can create complex lists of all sorts of objects, and then process them with minimal overhead.

It is true that in C you can simulate polymorphism using void pointers and doing a considerable amount of typecasting. While this has its advantages, it is not nearly as elegant a solution as is provided by C++, nor as powerful. While the simulation is possible, you cannot use a structure hidden within a void pointer without first casting it to be a pointer to a given structure. Therefore, you must have some way of knowing what the structure is behind any given void pointer. You lose the power of common protocols between objects and the power of directly accessing a pointer regardless of its declared type.

In an object-oriented language, a list can contain many different objects, provided they are derived from the same base class. In Smalltalk, all classes are derived ultimately from Object, therefore there is no need to create a special base class for container class purposes. In addition to this, Smalltalk contains several built-in container classes—OrderedCollection, Array, SortedCollection—and there is generally no need for additional classes of this type. In C++ and Pascal, however, there is the need for such constructions.

Suppose we want to have a list that stores employees and students of a school. We begin by defining a simple list, which stores something we will call a ListNode (*Figure 1.3*).

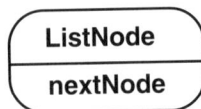

Figure 1.3 : ListNode.

Not much in it, and it doesn't look too effective, but it is. Our list will contain ListNodes. Well, they won't actually be ListNodes, but *derivatives* of ListNodes. Derive PERSON from ListNode, and you can now store both STUDENTs and EMPLOYEEs in the same list (*Figure 1.4*).

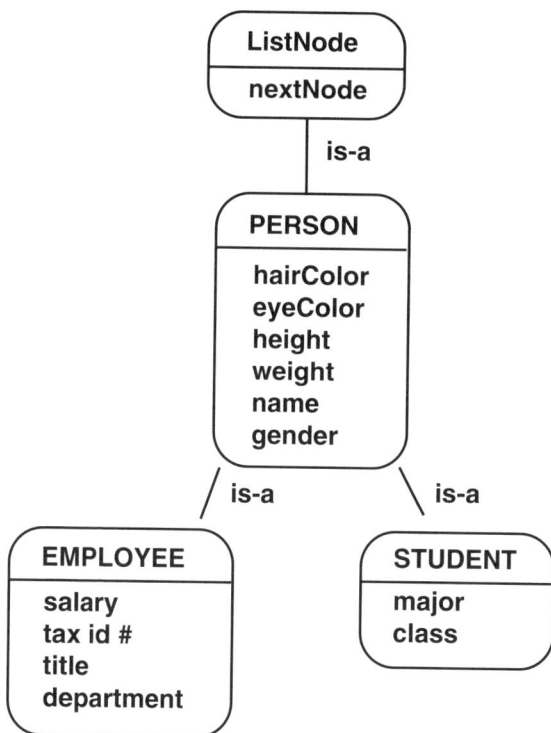

Figure 1.4 : ListNode Hierarchy.

Of course, now you have a list full of pointers to ListNodes! Getting at the actual class requires typecasting to the desired class (*Figure 1.5*).

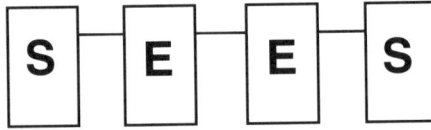

Figure 1.5 : (S)tudent & (E)mployee List.

Let's ask the list in *Figure 1.5* to give us the first thing in the list, which in this case is a STUDENT. Because the list only stores ListNodes, what you get is a pointer to a ListNode. No data, nothing specific to a student, just a simple data type. In order to look at the information as if it were a STUDENT, you typecast the returned pointer to be of type pointer to STUDENT. The same is true for EM-PLOYEE, or any other user-defined type derived from ListNode that is stored in the list.

The reason we can do this is because C++ and Borland's Turbo Pascal with Objects use a technique known as *late* (or sometimes run-time) *binding*. The data is not bound to the variable until run-time, and therefore no conflicts occur during compilation. When the source is compiled the value used to declare a pointer (usually a base class) is used to resolve that pointer.

For a pointer to be resolved, you only need to have a reference to the type it points to. The rules of object-oriented syntax allow you to set a pointer to a base class to point to any object that is derived from that class. This allows us to declare a pointer to Listdata, and point it at an instance of LISTDATA, PERSON, STUDENT or EMPLOYEE, or even all four (at different times, of course).

The only catch is this: When accessing members in a subclass, which don't exist in the base class through such a pointer, you must typecast the pointer to the type you are actually accessing, or the compiler will call your code an error.

If you think this through, it only makes sense. The compiler is a static thing. It doesn't trace the way your code executes, it only resolves references and generates machine code. If you told the compiler that your pointer was of type Listdata, and then point it at type STUDENT, the compiler won't complain, because it understands STUDENT is a type of Listdata.

But if you try to access the Grade member of that pointer, the compiler is not smart enough to realize that the Grade member belongs to the inherited class you're pointing to right now. If it could run through your code and execute it line-by-line, then it would be an interpreter, not a compiler.

So how do you get around this problem? Simple. Declare the pointer to point to a base class type, then write your code similar to *Listing 1.1*.

C++:

```
Listdata *lpNextPerson;        // Pointer to the next person in the list
...                            // Some code here...

Listdata = new Student();      // Create an empty student
                               // Here comes the typecast
```

```
((Student *)lpNextPerson)->Grade(13);   // Set the student's grade to 13.
```

OO Pascal:

```
Listdata^.NextPerson;                    // Pointer to the next person in the list
...                                      // Some code here

NextPerson := new(Student,Init);         // Create an empty Student
                                         // Here's the typecast...

(Student^)NextPerson^.Grade(11);         // Set the student's grade to 11.
```

Listing 1.1

The compiler knows it's okay to create new STUDENTs, and assign them to a LISTDATA pointer, but it doesn't know for sure that right now you are pointing at a STUDENT. You just told it that, for this member call, the pointer is indeed pointing to a STUDENT. Because the compiler now knows that you're talking about a STUDENT, it can provide the necessary reference to the student's Grade() member.

Warning: This method, while an integral part of both Turbo Pascal with Objects and C++ development, breaks the compiler's rules of safe typechecking. If you typecast the NextPerson pointer above to STUDENT, and it was actually pointing to an instance of TEACHER, the compiler wouldn't notice, because it doesn't know how your code executes, but you would corrupt your memory, and probably lock your computer.

In Smalltalk, typecasting is most frequently done through a method that begins with the mnemonic *as* and is followed by the name of the class to which you are typecasting. For example, '1' asNumber returns to you an instance of SmallInteger with the value of 1. Conversely, 1 asString returns to you the string '1'.

These methods are more complex than simply saying 'you now point to a class of this type,' as the actual conversion from one class to another is done inside these methods, but from a higher level it is just as elegant and simple—just say asClassName.

The compiler puts a reference to the method name in the compiled code that is resolved at run time by using tables that tell the executing program which copy of the method should be executed. Smalltalk is different in that it is an interpreted language. Methods are compiled when they are referenced during run time, cached for a period of time, and then released from memory. Instead of looking through tables for the correct method, the correct method to be executed has already been accessed through a call to it, and therefore it is directly executed.

It doesn't seem like we've gained anything, because you can typecast in C and get the same results as with C++. The power of polymorphism comes through the use of virtual and over-ridden methods, with which no typecasting is necessary. You can define a method in a base class, and then redefine it again in a subclass in order to implement more specific behavior.

For example, the hairColor method in PERSON simply returns the data member hairColor, but in another class called ME it might implement code that first checks what the date is and then returns either blonde or brown, because during the summer the sun lightens the hairColor of instances of ME and during the rest of the year the objects have a hairColor of brown. This is one of the most powerful aspects of the object-oriented paradigm.

CHAPTER 2
Classes and Instances

So far, we've talked about classes, but nothing about implementation or the creation of objects, or instances, without which you cannot do a whole lot. Many OO courses start by exploiting the parallels between classes and structures; this book will not. It is difficult enough to understand object-oriented concepts without clouding them with a structured view of the world. Too often, a structured view of object orientation obfuscates the object-oriented paradigm by confusing the student 'I could do that just as easily in [C... Pascal... Basic].'

While much of the actual code and implementation is based on a structured language—C++ uses the standard C language plus its extensions, Borland's Turbo Pascal with Objects uses standard Pascal plus Borland's Pascal extensions and its object extensions—the concepts that surround the object-oriented paradigm are very different from the one found in a structured environment. There are no such things as functions in the sense that a function exists as an individual entity in the procedural realm.

For instance, in a procedural environment you would create a function, called animalSpeak, which takes as a parameter an animal structure. The function writes to standard output a 'woof' for a dog, a 'meow' for a cat, or a 'tweet' for a bird.

In the object realm, each animal would have a method of the same name, and you would call on each animal to speak. Each animal's 'speech' method writes to standard output their own 'voice.' In this way, all functions are specific to a particular set of data members and cannot be used without being referenced through the class in which they are defined. An instance of a dog cannot use the cat's speech method, and vice-versa.

Although small object-oriented applications may have a module-like feel to them—several classes fit together into a more specific grouping—there is not a similar concept in the object-oriented paradigm. The complexity which with an object-oriented system fits together makes modules obselete and unnecessary.

A *class* is quite like a template, or more precisely, a definition. It defines the classes internal data members and holds methods that are specific to that definition. A class for a Screen might include data members such as coordinate system, background color, foreground color, current position, and its current cursor type. The methods that are defined for Screen would in some way manipulate one or more of its data members.

In a procedural language, you might implement a method called setCurrentPosition (aScreen, aPosition). In an object realm, you tell the Screen to set its current position to aPosition. Because in an object system you are talking directly to the Screen you want to manipulate, there is no need to pass around the Screen itself, as is done in a procedural environment.

In truth, the actual implementation of C++ passes as a parameter to every method the data member called *this*. *This* is a pointer to the instance of the class, and is invisible to the developer. You can access *this* in any method, and is often used to return a reference or pointer to the instance of the class back to the caller. This is because of the implementation of C++ as an extension of C.

An *instance* is the result of the creation of a class. In C and Pascal, the simple declaration of a pointer is not enough; you must allocate the memory for the pointer and assign it to a variable. The same is true for a class. You cannot simply declare a class and begin using it. Special allocation methods, called constructors, are used in order to insure that the proper variables have been initialized and memory allocated if necessary. Only after this method is called, whether explicitly or implicitly, can you begin using the methods defined for the manipulation of the object's data members.

Another important point is that while the methods are the same for every object created of a class, the data stored in that object is not necessarily the same.

For example, the class PERSON holds data members, and might even hold a class method species, which would return Homo sapien. Korey, Jeremy and Katherine are instances of the class PERSON. They are all people, and all contain the same data members, but the value of those data members are specific to the individual, or instance. The method species, however, always returns the same value for Korey, Jeremy or Katherine because it is specific to the class and not the instance. This type of method is known as a *class* method.

Smalltalk/V allows for the direct definition of class methods, while in C++ these would best be implemented by declaring the method to be static. In doing so, all instances of the class use the same copy of the method, and it could always return TRUE.

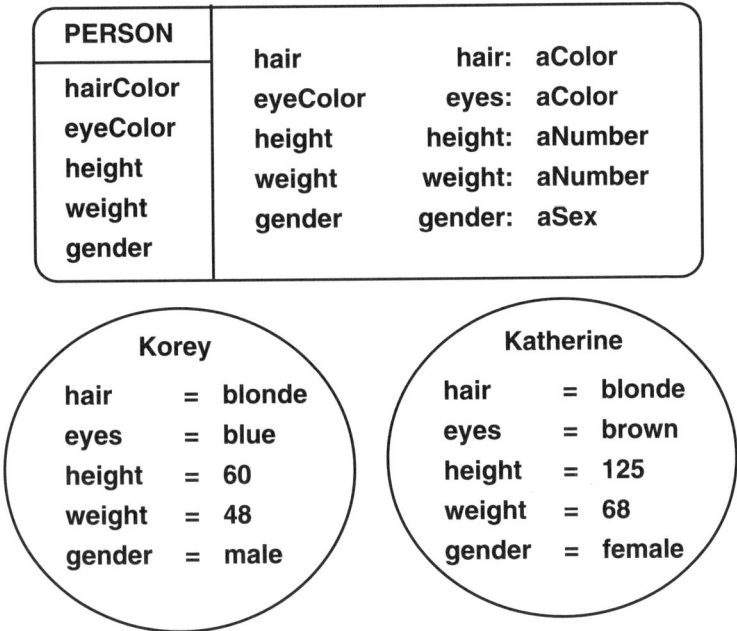

PERSON		
	hair	hair: aColor
hairColor	eyeColor	eyes: aColor
eyeColor	height	height: aNumber
height	weight	weight: aNumber
weight	gender	gender: aSex
gender		

Korey		
hair	=	blonde
eyes	=	blue
height	=	60
weight	=	48
gender	=	male

Katherine		
hair	=	blonde
eyes	=	brown
height	=	125
weight	=	68
gender	=	female

Figure 2.1 : Person Instances.

In *Figure 2.1*, the class PERSON is more detailed, as it includes the methods to the right of the definition. The left-hand column represents *get* access methods, and the right indicates *set* access methods. *get* methods are those that return to the caller the value of the data members, and *set* methods are those that set the value of a data member.

At this point, it is irrelevant what the language implementation is, it is the concept that is most important. The two bubbles below the class PERSON are instances of the class. They are two people, Korey and Katherine. Inside the bubble are the data members and their values as they pertain to each instance. You can see that they are completely different, as Korey and Katherine are two completely different instances of a person. When implemented, they will both use the same access methods to manipulate their data members, but the values returned and set will be different depending on who is calling the methods.

Listing 2.1 shows each language, the actual call, and the value returned.

Language		Actual call	Value returned
Smalltalk/V		Korey hair	blonde
		Katherine hair	blonde
C++		Katherine.eyes()	brown
		Korey.eyes()	blue
	or	Katherine->eyes()	brown
		Korey->eyes()	blue
OO Pascal		Korey.gender	male
		Katherine.gender	female
	or	Korey^.gender	male
		Katherine^.gender	female

Note: C++ / OOPascal have two ways of calling a method, depending on whether the variable name is a pointer to the instance or a satirically declared instance.

Listing 2.1

Each instance shares the same code for its methods, but its data members are specific to the individual. This is very different from the procedural realm, where you would need to pass a variable to a function in order to get to the data.

Building and Destroying Instances— Constructors and Destructors

The creation of classes in all languages is handled by a special method called a *constructor*. This method must be called before any other method can be used. A constructor initializes data members, allocating memory if necessary, and returns to you an instance of the class.

Its counterpart, the *destructor*, destroys the instance by de-allocating any memory allocated by the constructor and removes the ability to access the instance. This is handled differently in each language, but the concept is the same.

Smalltalk has no real destructor, although you can kill instances. All objects are garbage collected automatically for you when they are no longer referenced by any other object.

Although only Turbo Pascal with Objects requires an explicit constructor and destructor, it is a good idea in C++ to implement them. Advanced concepts such as inheritance and copy constructors will require them, and including them in your class, even if they are trivial and do absolutely nothing, is a good habit to practice. Smalltalk allows you to name constructors whatever you want. Turbo Pascal with Objects allows the same, but the constructor and destructor must be preceded by the keyword *constructor* and *destructor*, respectively (case is, of course, irrelevant in Turbo Pascal with Objects). C++ constructors are named according to the class's name. If the class name is PERSON, then the constructor is named PERSON() and the destructor is ~PERSON().

Creating classes using constructors is quite simple. *Listing 2.2* contains a table of constructor usage for each language, using both static and dynamic allocation.

Language	static	dynamic
C++	className variableName;	className * variableName = new className;
OOPascal	variableName.Init	variableName := New(className,Init)
Smalltalk		className new

Notes: **Init** is actually the name of the constructor you have defined. Smalltalk contains only one way to construct classes - dynamic, because all Smalltalk objects are pointers to an object.

Listing 2.2

As in any other language, if you do not assign the returning value of any of these calls to a variable, the returned value is lost.

In C++, using either the static or dynamic method of construction, the constructor is automatically called for you, unless when using the dynamic method you simply declare: className * varName. It would then become necessary to perform the second part of the construction as an explicit call: varName = **new** className.

The same is true in Turbo Pascal with Objects, where the declaration would be: varName : ^className, and then, varName := new(className, constructorName). Smalltalk also requires you to call a constructor, whether it be new, createMeAPerson, or some other name which is more suited to your application. These calls are the method in which a class is instantiated, and you receive an object with which to work.

A developer can also implement a special kind of constructor, known as a *copy constructor*. This constructor, instead of initializing data members and the like, does exactly what you would think it does—it makes a copy of the object passed to it, and returns that copy to the caller. A copy constructor for person written in C++ might be written as shown in *Listing 2.3*.

```
class PERSON
{
     ..... // data members and other constructors
     PERSON( PERSON &aPerson);
};
```

Note: The & operator in C++ represents a reference to an instance. This is similar to a pointer, but much safer and much more efficient.

This type of constructor is invoked in the following manner:

```
 PERSON aPerson();
... fill the data members of aPerson
PERSON aPerson2(aPerson);
```

Listing 2.3

What is returned to you from aPerson2 is an exact copy of aPerson.

There are two types of copy constructors: a *shallow copy* and *deep copy*. A shallow copy assigns the values in aPerson to the data members in aPerson2. Normally, this would not cause problems, but if there are arrays, or pointers involved, this means that the developer must be aware that aPerson and aPerson2, after aPerson2 is instantiated, will be accessing the same variables. If aPerson changes a data member that happens to be a pointer to a character array, then the value in aPerson2 is also changed.

A deep copy makes complete duplicates of all aPerson's data members and then assigns them to the aPerson2's data members. A change to one will not affect the other after the creation of aPerson2. The differences here, if ignored, can cause problems in applications, so developers need to be aware of them in order to correctly use the right type of copy, if one is being used.

Defining Classes in the OO Languages

Now you understand the basic differences between classes and instances of classes, and you know how to create and destroy them, but you still don't know how to define them!

We will define the class PERSON, and the methods shown in *Figure 2.1* for all three of our OO languages in *Listing 2.4*. Keywords will be shown in bold, in order to emphasize the necessary syntax.

C++

Note: Data members and methods are declared either *private, public* or *protected* in C++. Private data members and methods mean nothing outside this class has access to them, public means that anyone can have access to them, and protected means that only class methods, and the methods of classes that inherit from this class have access to them.

```
class Person
{
private:
    char        hairColor[10];
    char        eyeColor[10];
    int   Weight;
    int   Height;
    int   Gender;


public:
    Person();       // this is the constructor
    ~Person();      // this is the destructor

    char * hair();          // "Get" for hairColor data member
    char * eyes();          // "Get" for eyeColor data member
    int     weight();       // "Get" for weight data member
    int     height();       // "Get" for height data member
    int     gender();       // "Get" for gender data member
    void    hair(char *);   // "Set" for hairColor data member
    void    eyes(char *);   // "Set" for eyeColor data member
    void    weight(int);    // "Set" for weight data member
    void    height(int);    // "Set" for height data member
    void    gender(int);    // "Set" for gender data member
};
```

* * * * *

OO Pascal

```
TYPE
Person = Object
    hairColor : string;
    eyeColor : string;
    weight    : integer;
    height    : integer;
    gender    : integer;
```

32

```
Constructor Init;          (* this is the constructor *)
Destructor Done;           (* this is the destructor *)

Function hair: string;     (* "Get" for hairColor data member *)
Function eyes: string;     (* "Get" for eyeColor data member *)
Function weight: integer;  (* "Get" for weight data member *)
Function height: integer;  (* "Get" for height data member *)
Function gender: integer;  (* "Get" for gender data member *)

Procedure hair( color: string)    (* "Set" for HairColor data member *)
Procedure weight( amt: integer);  (* "Set" for weight data member *)
Procedure height( amt: integer);  (* "Set" for height data member *)
Procedure gender( sex: integer);  (* "Set" for gender data member *)
end.
```

✱ ✱ ✱ ✱ ✱

Smalltalk / V

Note: Smalltalk classes would be implemented in a Class Browser and the process is best left for other books to explain, what follows is the definition as it appears in a file if you choose File It Out from the menu. The methods would, of course, be followed by the implementation.

```
Object subclass: Person
    instanceVariableNames: ' hairColor eyeColor weight height gender '
    classVariableNames: ''
    poolDictionaries: '' !
```

!Person class methods!

Note: Because this class is practicing inheritance already, it doesn't need a constructor. It can use its parent's constructor new.

!Person methods!

```
hair        " Get the hairColor data member "
    < some code goes here >!!
eyes        " Get the eyeColor data member "
    < some code goes here >!!
weight      " Get the weight data member "
    < some code goes here >!!
height      " Get the height data member "
```

```
    < some code goes here >!!
gender        " Get the gender data member "
    < some code goes here >!!

hair: aString            " Set the hairColor data member "
    < some code goes here >!!
eyes: aString            " Set the eyeColor data member "
    < some code goes here >!!
weight: anInteger        " Set the weight data member "
    < some code goes here >!!
height: anInteger        " Set the height data member "
    < some code goes here >!!
gender: anInteger        " Set the gender data member "
    < some code goes here >!!
```

Defining the methods is simply a matter of syntax. Examples in all three languages follow.

C++

```
char * Person::hair()                 // method definition
{
        return hair;                  // return the  data member
};

void Person::hair( char * pszHairColor)   // method definition
{
     strcpy(hairColor, pszHairColor);   // Set the data  member's value
};

Person::Person()                      // constructor  definition
{
     hairColor[0] = '\0';             // set data members to nulls
     eyeColor[0] = '\0';
     weight = height = gender = 0;
};

Person::~Person()                     // destructor  definition
{                                     // does nothing, no memory
                                            allocated
}
```

Note: Constructors and destructors cannot specify return values in C++.

* * * * *

OO Pascal

```
Function Person.hair : string;          // method definition
Begin
    hair := hairColor;                  // return data member
end.

Procedure Person.hair ( newColor : string);   // method definition
Begin
    hairColor := newColor;              // set data member
end.

Constructor Person.init;                // constructor definition
Begin
    hairColor := '';                    // set all data members
    eyeColor := '';                     // to nulls
    weight := 0;
    height := 0;
    gender := 0;
end.

Destructor Person.Done;                 // destructor definition
Begin           end.                    // does nothing, but
                                        // good habit
```

* * * * *

Smalltalk/V

```
hair                                    // method
    ^hairColor                          // return data member

hair : aColor                           // method
    hairColor := aColor                 // set the data member
```

Note: Smalltalk/V constructors can be named anything, and are normally class methods. If you need to initialize data members, it can be done in the constructor, or in an instance method initialize, which seems to be the standard name.

Listing 2.4

35

The actual implementation looks much like the structured languages upon which C++ and Borland's Turbo Pascal with Objects were built off of, but the concepts encased in the code are anything but procedural.

Defining Methods

The actual implementation of the methods are standard to the language, returning or setting data members in the same way that variables are treated in C or Pascal. There are some additional syntactical extensions to C++ and Borland's Turbo Pascal with Objects are important to the language, but are not so important to understand the object-oriented paradigm.

In general, there are specific ways to define methods using the extensions, and the rest of the implementation relies on the base language C or Pascal. In C++, the **scope resolution operator**, is used to define a method outside the class definition, and in Borland's Turbo Pascal with Objects a period is used to indicate a method definition. Both use the same syntax otherwise, **className** operator **method-name**.

Discovering Objects

There are many methodologies that can help you do analysis and design of an object-oriented application: Coad/Yourdon, Booch, CRC cards, and a host of others. We will discuss analysis and design methodologies and present what has worked best for us, but which one is best for you is your decision.

It all comes down to the same beginning—**find**ing the objects in your application. The most basic way to find objects is to look for the nouns. It's that simple. What is generally different about the methodologies, aside from their notations, is the way in which they find nouns that map to objects in the system. Finding the nouns, which will become objects, is the first and probably most important part of analysis. These objects are often found in such nouns as **menu**, **file**, **database**, **customer** and **service**.

Consider writing an application for a fruit stand. You have to model the fruit stand, so where do you begin? Envision a fruit stand, and then start writing down the nouns that come to mind when describing the fruit stand: fruit, stand, baskets, bags, cash, employees and customers are a good start. Now take a good look at those nouns. Are there any that seem to be of the same general category? Employees and customers are both people; the stand, baskets and bags are all equipment of some sort.

The classification you put the nouns under becomes a base class, with the nouns becoming subclasses of those base classes.

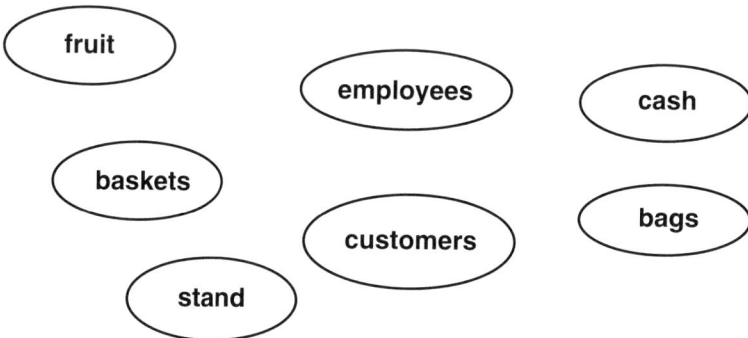

Figure 2.2 : Nouns in Fruit Stand Business.

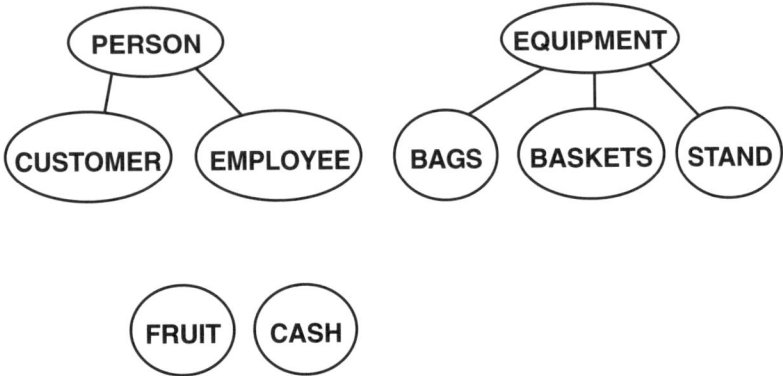

Figure 2.3: Class from Nouns in Figure 2.2.

Figure 2.2 shows the model as initially conceived; *Figure 2.3* shows the model after grouping and the creation of base and subclasses. This is where the reuse of code comes in, and the power of object-oriented development begins to emerge. Subclasses inherit the methods of their parents, which means that you only have to write the code one time, and it can be used repeatedly by many different subclasses. Why reinvent the wheel repeatedly when you can write it once and use it efficiently? Subclassing is a process borne of inheritance.

Virtual Methods

Equipment is the base class for three other classes in our model. Businesses use a depreciation amount for equipment in figuring their taxes. So it makes sense that the class would have as a data member a depreciation variable, or at the very least a method that would figure the depreciation of the equipment for us.

A problem arises, in that the stand and the baskets will depreciate differently. So we've written code that might work for one subclass, but not the other. Not to worry, object-oriented languages allow us to use *virtual methods* in order to overcome this problem. Both C++ and Turbo Pascal with Objects require the keyword virtual in the declaration of such methods, while Smalltalk/V assumes that all over-ridden methods are virtual.

The method depreciation will be implemented in the base class, but it will be a virtual method, meaning that each subclass will implement the method also according to its own needs. Does it seem like we're rewriting code, and that it's useless? Perhaps, but this implementation allows us to establish a common protocol among all subclasses, which in more complex examples will allow for some really neat things to happen.

Common protocol across classes is the basis for many advanced concepts, not simply object-oriented concepts. OSI (Open Systems Interface) is a seven-layer protocol that defines how a system must act and define data in order to interface with other systems that are not necessarily of the same hardware type. OSI will allegedly allow Mac computers to talk to VAX systems, UNIX systems and PCs.

This standard defines a common protocol across systems in order to allow for all systems to decode information sent by other systems. By following that protocol, it becomes irrelevant where data comes from, as long as the protocol to access it is consistent across systems. It is somewhat analogous to standard data file formats, such as dBase, FoxPro and others. By defining a common interface to an object, messaging becomes standardized and more complex systems can be built.

In *Figure 1.5*, we created a list of students and employees. Suppose we change the contents of the list to include students and teachers, and added another data member which for students held the classes they were enrolled in and for teachers held the classes they taught.

Now suppose we want to go through the list and find all students and teachers who either are in or teach a particular class. We could review the list and check each person to see if they are a student or a teacher and then check to see if they match the criteria. But, that would violate the paradigm, because we should not have to find out what type of person they are at all.

If we implement a virtual method in PERSON called match, then every person in the list would know how to respond to that method. If each subclass of PERSON implements that method according to its internal data, then we will be able to call upon a match with a course name and get the right data returned to us.

CHAPTER 3
Inheritance

Inheritance relates directly to the process of subclassing, or creating classes that are derived from a base class. C++ is the only language of the three we have been discussing that allows the uses of multiple inheritance. It is not a widely used technique, but in certain situations it is a magnificent tool to use.

When you create a class by deriving from another class, the new class is said to inherit the attributes and methods of the class from which it is derived. With this terminology, you can think of the base class as being a parent and its subclasses being children. Parents pass on their genetic traits to children through their genes, and children are generally recognized through the traits of their parents. Both attributes and behaviors are attributable to lineage in human beings.

The same is true in the programming realm, with a slight twist. Children are more like clones of their parents, with additional behavior and attributes coming from somewhere else. Unlike human children, class children inherit all of their parent's attributes and behaviors (there are certain exceptions to this rule in C++). The children have access to all of the parents attributes and methods, and their children have access to all of their attributes and methods as well as the original parent, or grandparent. This hierarchy allows for specialization.

Reusability of Code Through Inheritance

Inheritance is the mechanism that allows object-oriented code to be reused. Most people seem to believe that by reuse we mean that you can simply pop the code in and go, with no additional development time. This is sometimes the case, but not always. Usually the standard ADTs, such as stacks, queues, and those that are commonly known as container classes are simply a matter of pulling one off the shelf and plugging it into an application.

However, more often you will derive from some already implemented class and specialize according to the application's needs. There is already a huge commercial market in tools, often called class libraries, which are geared toward developers. These libraries contain already implemented classes that can be used by developers in order to aid the software development process. These tools range from container classes, to huge database systems, communication packages, and graphical interface libraries which allow you to use the same code across platforms in your development efforts.

In *Chapter 1* we defined a PERSON class, that held basic information about a person. It is generic, and isn't really much use in a real application. But by deriving from it (*Chapter 2*) we created more specific classes, STUDENT and EMPLOYEE. The efficiency here is that PERSON had to be implemented only once.

In a structured implementation, the code relating to PERSON may very well have been implemented twice, once for STUDENT and once for EMPLOYEE. The object-oriented paradigm encourages you to write it once and use it again and again.

The exploitation of common attributes among entities allows for the use of inheritance to work for the developer. It should be noted that these advantages do not come purely through the use of object technology. Through the analysis and design process, classes will tend to crop up that have much in common, and differ in a few areas. If the developer does not find these cases and exploit them, you have gained little.

These classes are prime candidates for subclassing. When you begin writing the same code, the same attributes, or the same responsibilities over and over, you have walked into the middle of an excellent candidate for subclassing of a base class. Not only does this save development time, it saves testing time as well. A well-tested and quality-assured base class provides a solid foundation for you to build off of, without wondering if it's going to work, or if the code was copied correctly, or any number of the procedural realm worries. If you're implementing the same code repeatedly, and you're allegedly writing an object-oriented system, stop what you're doing. Examine what you are writing, and how it fits in with the class you are writing. Check its parent (if there is one), and other classes in the system to see if there is a better place from which to implement the code one time, and still have the access you require.

Implementing this is not much more complicated than it sounds. We already have the methods defined for PERSON in *Figure 2.1*, but we have nothing defined for STUDENT or EMPLOYEE. This is done in *Figure 3.1*.

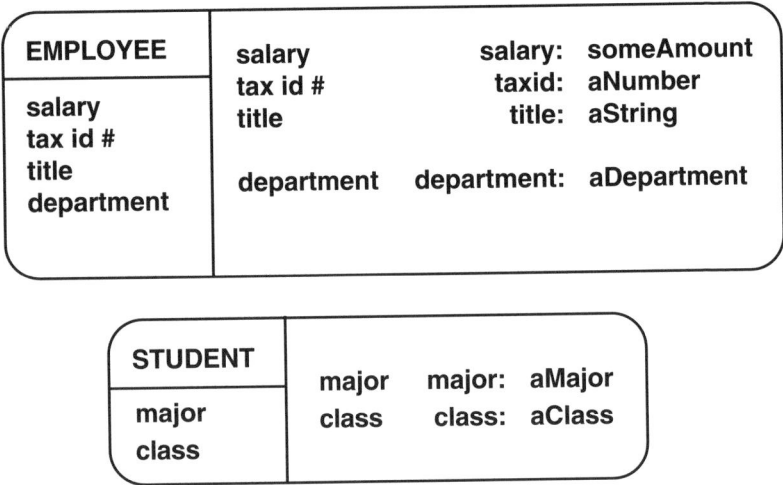

EMPLOYEE	salary tax id # title	salary: someAmount taxid: aNumber title: aString
salary tax id # title department	department	department: aDepartment

STUDENT	major class	major: aMajor class: aClass
major class		

Figure 3.1 : Employee and Student Classes.

Accessing Inherited Methods/Data Members

Remember now that both STUDENT and EMPLOYEE are merely extensions of PERSON and contain all the data members that PERSON does and have access to PERSON's methods. So how does a STUDENT get at its hair color? The same way it accesses any of its specific data members. If Korey is a STUDENT, then Korey.hair() retrieves his hairColor just as it did when Korey was a PERSON. The same for EMPLOYEE, and any other subclass of PERSON.

This assumes, of course, that the inheritance being used is single inheritance, (i.e., that a class has only one parent). This, of course, is only a problem in C++, because it is the only one of the three explored in this book that allows multiple inheritance. Dealing with this issue is solved in quite a simple way, and will be discussed in a later section.

When you call Korey.hair() in your code, the compiler takes over at compile time and attempts to find the method by walking through STUDENT hierarchy. If it does not find the method it will issue an error. Smalltalk/V works the same way. The only difference is that because Smalltalk is interpreted, you won't find out if the method is not defined anywhere in the hierarchy until you attempt to use the class.

Now that we have defined subclasses of PERSON, we can show you how polymorphism and typecasting actually works. Let's suppose we have the list shown in *Figure 3.2.*

Figure 3.2 : (S)tudents & (E)mployees List.

What is actually stored in the list are pointers to several instances of PERSON. Suppose that we want to iterate over the list and retrieve every PERSON that has brown hair. We walk through the list as we would any other list, asking every node to return hairColor. If it is brown, we do something with it. What we do with it is irrelevant, as it is the act of finding out if the PERSON's hairColor is brown that is important here.

Even though the first node is a STUDENT and the second node is an EMPLOYEE, they both know how to respond to the message hairColor, because they are both derived from PERSON, who implemented it. This is sometimes called the "substitutability" of children for their parents. In short, any place you declare a PERSON, you can substitute a STUDENT, or an EMPLOYEE, and as long as you are accessing inherited methods, the software system will react the same.

Now suppose that what we did when we found a node that contained a PERSON derivative that had hairColor equal to brown was to store it in another list in order to process it after we have all people with brown hair. We simply add it to another PERSON list. Now we want to do something to it, but what we want to do is different for a STUDENT than it is for an EMPLOYEE.

In order to properly process each node in the list, we must first cast the PERSON to the appropriate subclass. In Smalltalk this is unnecessary; simply access the node as the correct subclass and proceed. However, in C++ and Turbo Pascal with Objects this is not the case. If we have a current pointer in this new list, and we want to cast the first one to a STUDENT, we would do as shown in *Listing 3.1*.

```
C++                    STUDENT * temp;
                       temp = (STUDENT *) list->currentNode
       ( where currentNode is a pointer to the current node in the list )

OO Pascal              temp : ^STUDENT;
                       temp := (STUDENT^) list^.currentNode
```

Listing 3.1

Now we can access temp as a STUDENT. If the currentNode was an EMPLOYEE, we would simply replace the STUDENT types with EMPLOYEE with the same results. This typecasting is a part of polymorphism. How you determine what type of node you actually have is different in each language. Smalltalk uses classification methods that in the base class return false and for each type of subclass return true if the class is the type we are asking for. For example :

```
PERSON      >> isStudent returns false
PERSON      >> isEmployee returns false
STUDENT     >> isStudent returns true
EMPLOYEE    >> isEmployee returns true
```

You need not implement isEmployee for STUDENT, or isStudent for EMPLOYEE because the subclasses will automatically inherit the given methods from the base class and because they return false they are already returning the correct value. In C++ and Turbo Pascal with Objects, you can implement the same type of methods with the same results. Or, you can define a generic processing method in the base class, which for a STUDENT and EMPLOYEE may be over-ridden to do completely separate processes. This allows you to process both STUDENTs and EMPLOYEEs without ever knowing which one is which.

This is truly the power of data encapsulation, polymorphism, and inheritance combined. If this were to be implemented in a procedural language, separate procedures would be required for some STUDENT structure and some EMPLOYEE structure, and it would further be necessary to distinguish the type of the node before any processing could begin. With object technology, you can simply say:

```
for each node in the list
    if hairColor is brown
        that node do aMethod
```

As long as aMethod is defined in both classes, whether it be by simply defining it separately in each, or by only defining it in the base class, or by declaring it a virtual method, this type of iteration and processing is possible.

Single and Multiple Inheritance

There are many situations in which a developer would make use of inheritance. One reason, is to prevent the replication of the same code. A second reason, is to provide for many different classes a common protocol.

In earlier sections, lists were described that held different class types derived from the same base class. In the discussion of C++ and Turbo Pascal with Objects, reference was made to a common virtual method called process. Process provides a common protocol across classes that allows the developer to treat different classes as though they were the same, without having the overhead of checking the type of the class before processing.

Any discussion on multiple inheritance will be solely based on C++ code, because Turbo Pascal with Objects and Smalltalk do not support multiple inheritance. All three languages support single inheritance.

The difference is small. In single inheritance, you create a subclass from a single base class. With multiple inheritance, you derive a subclass from two or more base classes, thereby providing the class with access to two or more class' data and methods.

Where would this be useful? Most OO languages manage the concept of streams (read stream, a write stream, and a read/write stream), usually on files. In Smalltalk, a read/write stream, a stream that allows simultaneous reading and writing using the same stream, is implemented by deriving from one of the classes and reimplementing the other classes data and methods in the subclass. In C++, a read/write stream (fstream) is derived from both a read stream (ifstream) and a write stream (ofstream). This allows for the most efficient reuse of code.

Consider the case of a student employee who needs both the attributes of STUDENT and EMPLOYEE in a single class. Only in C++ can you implement this new subclass without duplicating existing code. There is not a huge number of cases where you would want to use multiple inheritance, but there are cases when it would save you development time in doing so.

Listing 3.2 shows the syntax for single and multiple inheritance, and Figure 3.3 shows a diagram of what multiple inheritance might look like.

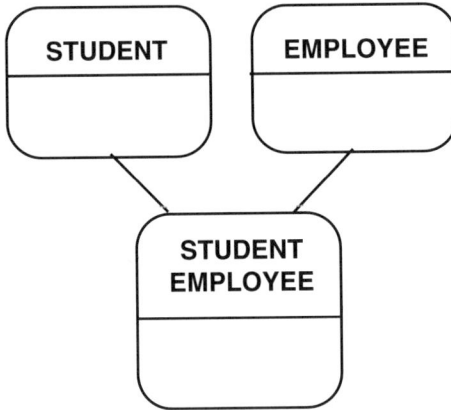

Figure 3.3 Multiple Inheritance Hierarchy

The syntax for single inheritance is as follows :

C++

```
class subclass : public baseclass
{ ... // class definition as before
};
```

Note: The keyword *public* may be replaced by *protected* or *private*. Only C++ allows you to define the access of data members, methods and derivations.

OO Pascal

```
subclass = Object( baseclass)
... (* definition as before *)
end.
```

Smalltalk

```
baseclass subclass: #subclass
" definition as before "
```

Note: The keyword *subclass* may be replaced by *variableByteSubclass* or *variableSubclass*. Only Smalltalk allows you to define different types of subclasses according to the type of data being stored in the class.

The syntax for multiple inheritance in C++ follows :

class subclass : **public** baseclass1, **public** baseclass2, ..., **public** baseclassN

Listing 3.2

Note that in *Figure 3.3* the STUDENT-EMPLOYEE is attached to both the EMPLOYEE and the STUDENT. This demonstrates that it receives the attributes and abilities of both classes in addition to any others we might define for this new class.

You may be wondering how you access a method implemented in the base class that is also implemented in the subclass, such as in the case of a STUDENT-EMPLOYEE. You don't want to remove the process of a student from STUDENT or an employee from EMPLOYEE, so you have redefined (over-ridden) the method in the new subclass. Suppose you want to call on the process method for STUDENT from a STUDENT-EMPLOYEE. *Listing 3.3* contains a table of the calls to do this in each language.

Language	Call
C++	baseclass::process();
OO Pascal	baseclass.process; or baseclass->process()
Smalltalk	super process

Listing 3.3

Note that earlier there were two ways to call a method in C++ and Turbo Pascal with Objects depending on whether you were using dynamically allocated or static variables. Here, C++ gives you only one way to access the method.

With multiple inheritance in C++, you use the same technique to access methods named in both base classes, to insure that you have called the correct method.

Overloaded Member Functions

Overloaded methods (overloading=static polymorphism) are methods with the same name that handle processing of different data types within the same class.

For example, our STUDENT class may have a method addGrade(int grade), which adds to a student's grades and computes their GPA using an integer-based grading system. But perhaps another professor doesn't give numerical grades, and wants to use the standard A,B,C grading scale. Instead of writing an entirely new method, we can use the same method name, and just pass it a different parameter: addGrade(char grade).

The processing is different, but we don't need to worry during processing whether the professor uses a numerical or character-based grading system. This is known as *function overloading*. Only C++ handles this concept directly within the class. Turbo Pascal with Objects does not handle overloading, and Smalltalk handles the concept in an entirely different manner. Smalltalk simply converts the passed parameter to the correct type, and if necessary writes the conversion method for the class.

For example, almost all classes in Smalltalk use the conversion asString. This is especially useful when using the debugger, or printing the result of instance creation.

Using the same example above, Smalltalk would have one method that looked like this:

(for class STUDENT)

pseudo-code :
        addGrade: aGrade
                change aGrade to an integer and add it to
                the cumulativeGPA variable
actual code:
        addGrade: aGrade
            cumulativeGPA add: aGrade asInteger

The asInteger could just as easily be asCharacter, and it is irrelevant which one it is. If the aGrade parameter is already an integer, there is no conversion, if it is a character, the class Character would need to contain the method asInteger, which would in some way return a representation of aGrade as an integer value. This concept is used quite often in C++, especially in reference to constructors and operators.

Operator overloading is handled by both C++ and Smalltalk, although in Smalltalk there truly is no such thing as an 'operator' because even base data types are represented as objects in Smalltalk. To overload an operator in C++, you use the following syntax:

        returntype operator operatorName (arguments)

For example, to overload the addition operator for STUDENT so that it adds a class to the student's list of classes, you would write the following method for class STUDENT:

```
STUDENT operator + ( aCourse * newCourse );

STUDENT operator + (char * newCourseName);
```

Note: The second method is exactly like the first, except that it takes a different parameter type. The first one takes a new course instance, and the second takes a character string with the class name as a parameter. The second one might simply use the class name to create a new instance of course inside the method body, and continue processing exactly as the first one does. The point is that operators can be overloaded operators and methods, both within the same class.

CHAPTER 4
Data Encapsulation

I sent a copy of this book to the printer on our server, and it printed. Not amazing, you say? Think about the process.

Somehow the data contained in this book needed to be encapsulated and sent to the printer, over a LAN to the server, from the server through the parallel port and finally to the printer where it is printed. You do not have to know in what form the data was stored while it was being sent through the network to the printer. You do not even have to know in what form the data is stored on your hard drive. You only have to know how to access it by sending commands to it.

The standard File menu contains the option Open. This command, FileOpen is sent to the system, which sends the open to a file and the file is opened and read into your word processor. You don't need to know how it was stored or loaded, you only need to know the commands necessary to perform these actions. This, basically is *data encapsulation*.

Definition of Data Encapsulation

Data encapsulation, or data hiding as it is sometimes called, is a technique that abstracts data and allows you to manipulate that data without ever knowing how it is being stored, or even as what type the data is stored. Whether you store your data as strings or integers, user defined types or base data types is irrelevant if you properly encapsulate your data. This is often done to save storage space or memory and to enhance performance.

Suppose we have a list of Customers and a list of Orders. Suppose a Customer stores a list of Orders, and an Order knows who its owning Customer is. Instead of storing the owning Customer in Order as an actual pointer or reference to the instance of the owning Customer, we might choose to store this data member as an integer, and place in that data member the customer number of the owning Customer. This decreases the amount of space needed during instantiation, manipulation and storage.

This is an important function of encapsulation. As long as we are sure to have a method within Order that can give us the instance of the owning Customer, given a customer number, we need not worry whether or not the data member is an actual customer, customer number, or even the name of the customer.

Implementation of Encapsulation

In order to properly encapsulate your data, it is important to define what are known as *accessor methods*, that is, methods that are designed and implemented specifically to manipulate the data members of a given object. They may be simply *set* or *get* standard convention methods, or they may be more complex, such as in the case of encryption coupled with encapsulation. Whatever the case, data encapsulated without accessor methods to manipulate it defeats the purpose of encapsulation.

This level of abstraction is particularly thorough in Smalltalk/V. A pure OO environment, you are abstracted to the level of knowing at the very most that the data is stored as pointers somewhere. But you have no access to that storage scheme, only to the data members through accessor methods. Only C++ can come close to this type of abstraction when full use is made of *private, protected* and *public* keywords applied to data members and methods, or to the base class name in class definitions.

In Smalltalk/V, you can prevent direct manipulation of variables by not defining accessor methods for those variables. This is not a purist approach, but it simulates the private keyword used in C++ to prevent subclasses from accessing data members directly. These keywords define the access all other classes have to the data within the defined class. Borland's Turbo Pascal with Objects does not have such a scheme, and while it simulates data abstraction through the definition of accessor methods, the developer is in no way forced to use or write them. In many cases, encapsulation in this language tends to disintegrate for lack of enforcement.

Examples of Encapsulation

In Smalltalk/V, all data members are private to their owning class. For example, if class X has the instance variables xName and xPhone, no other class may have access to those variables except through the use of accessor methods. Accessor methods commonly take the following form in Smalltalk/V:

standard "Set" accessor method
instanceVariableName: newValue
     instanceVariableName := newValue

standard "Get" accessor method
instanceVariableName
     ^instanceVariableName

In C++, the keyword private insures that no other classes may have access to the data members except through access methods implemented for those data members.

```
class X
{
private:
    xName;
    xPhone;
public:
    returnType xName();     // standard "Get" accessor method
    void xName( newValue); // standard "Set" accessor method
};
```

Subclasses of class X in C++ can have their access changed depending on their declaration: They also may have private, public or protected access to the base classes Public data members.

This sounds rather confusing, but let's take it from the viewpoint of (a) the class developer, and (b) the class user (who is developing subclasses).

A: The class developer is writing a class called Screen. He wants to abstract the text-mode screen of a color monitor. He decides that the class header would look like the code in *Listing 4.1.*

```
class Screen{

protected:
        int width;              // Width of the screen.
        int height;             // Height of the screen.
        int CurrX;              // Current width position.
        int CurrY;              // Current height position.

private:
        int ForeColor;          // Foreground color.
        int BackColor;          // Background color.

public:
        Screen();               // Constructor.
        ~Screen(){}             // Destructor.
        SetForeGround(int color);   // Used to set the foreground color.
        SetBackGround(int color);   // Used to set the background color.
        SetWidth(int Width);    // Used to set the screen width.
        SetHeight(int Height);  // Used to set the screen height.
        MoveCurrPos
            (int newX, int newY);   // Set CurrX and CurrY to values.
        Write(char *lpszString);    // Write lpszString at current pos.
        Clear();                // Clear the screen and re-initialize.
};
```

Listing 4.1

Suppose this developer spent considerable time writing the code to set the foreground and background colors at the hardware level. Using anything other than his functions to change colors would set the Screen object out of sync with the actual monitor (if you were to change the color elsewhere, how would the Screen object know what the new color was?).

Therefore, he made the ForeColor and BackColor members private. This says: 'NO ONE may access these variables!'. But, planning for the future, and 43 line screens, he made the other variables protected. Protected means 'Only people who inherit from me can access these variables!'. So, the developer creating subclasses of Screen can have their subclasses directly manipulate Screen's variables (this is not a purist OO way of doing things, but it is readily accepted as a fact in C++ programming).

B: So, the class user decides to inherit from Screen. He must decide what type of access his child class needs. If he doesn't need to directly manipulate Screen's variables, he could declare his subclass (we'll call it window):

```
class Window: private Screen
{
    ...
};
```

But if he wants to make Window use Screen's variables directly, he can make his declaration:

```
class Window: public Screen
{
    ...
};
```

Last, if he wants to manipulate Screen's variables directly, but doesn't think classes that inherit from window will need to, he can make his declaration:

```
class Window: protected Screen
{
    ...
};
```

In Borland Pascal with Objects, you can simulate data encapsulation by defining accessor methods, but there is no technique currently available that allows you to enforce encapsulation.

Error Checking / Handling

A major advantage of data encapsulation is the error checking and handling that can be done to insure that the caller does not have to worry about bad data being returned to them. Extensive error checking inside of an accessor methods insures that the caller is being returned a valid piece of data. There is no need, indeed it is inefficient, to check and recheck values being returned from a call if the implementation is done properly.

The class' methods are responsible for error checking. It is not the caller's responsibility to worry about data validation. Indeed, if encapsulation is implemented correctly there should be no way for the caller to know whether data is valid. The class must insure that the data is consistently valid.

In C++, you can extend this process even further because you can over-ride standard functions and operators. By over-riding the new operator (used to dynamically allocate pointers to classes and other data types) you can embed debugging capabilities exception handling within your class to further validate data. Most errors are caused by pointer problems, and by embedding logic within operators that handle the allocation and deallocation of memory, you can more easily track these problems.

In Smalltalk/V, you can use similar processes in order to debug and track problems. In Borland's Turbo Pascal with Objects, tracking through the constructor and destructor is probably the best way to implement additional error detection and handling, because you cannot over-ride operators in that language.

CHAPTER 5
Data Abstraction

Data abstraction is the process of simplifying, or abstracting, and grouping data and operations related to that data into a single entity called a class. In a procedural language, you define a type, and then create functions or procedures to handle the manipulation of that data. In an object-oriented language, you create a single new data type that can be manipulated through the use of its methods.

But abstraction is more than just making classes, it is also the process of simplifying your data while meeting the needs of your application. You keep only the data that is relevant to the class, and nothing else. This makes classes and methods often times less complex than procedural types and functions, making it easier to implement. This is the process by which a PERSON is created from EMPLOYEES and CUSTOMERS. The common data members and methods, such as name, address, and phone number, are placed in their own class. This approach reduces redundancy throughout applications, because common code is not implemented over and over again.

Data Abstraction and Generic Code

Making data simpler and easier to implement is a matter of abstraction, and also of reuse. If you look closely at the lists programmers write, they all have common aspects, with the only real difference being the data that is stored. Stacks, lists, queues, trees and arrays (often called container classes in C++) all have a common protocol, which in procedural languages is implemented time and time again according to the data being stored in them. If we abstract these fundamental data types into classes that contain only relevant data and the methods relevant to that data we end up with classes that can be reused efficiently.

The abstract data types are generic in that the data that is stored within them is irrelevant, unlike in procedural programming. These pieces of generic code save development time because they only have to be implemented once, or retrieved from an outside source, and then can be used with any type of user-defined data types.

Simplification of Code

Abstraction can simplify code by removing extraneous data not directly relevant to any given class. A list class has generic listNodes as data, and perhaps a size variable. A listNode has at the bare minimum a pointer to the next node in the list, and usually nothing else. It contains only methods relevant to operations that would be performed relevant to a list (e.g., getting the next node in the list, setting the next node in the list, and perhaps a virtual method called match or process, or both).

These two methods are related to the list in that we might want to iterate over the list and process data or find data within the list. The methods are purely virtual, which means that they have no code and cannot be used at the level they are defined as purely virtual. By virtue of a class having at least one purely virtual method, it is known as an *abstract class*.

An abstract class is one that cannot be used to create objects. It is used to establish a common protocol, as a base class, and to provide generic data nodes within container classes. This is accomplished in C++ and Smalltalk/ V through methods, and is not available in Borland's Turbo Pascal with Objects. *Listing 5.1* demonstrates how to implement an abstract class in each Smalltalk/V and C++.

C++

```
class abstractPerson
{
public:
        char * lpszName;
        abstractPerson();          // constructor
        ~abstractPerson();         // destructor
        virtual void processPerson() = 0;
};
```

Smalltalk/V

```
Object subclass: #abstractPerson
                instanceVariableNames: 'name'
                classVariableNames: ''
                poolDictionaries: ''

processPerson
                ^self implementedBySubclass
```

Listing 5.1

In Smalltalk/V, the method implemented BySubclass is inherited from Object, and ends in an error to the effect of "Subclass should have implemented." This tells us that the class is abstract, and that the class should not be instantiated. In C++, the keyword virtual is used again, but the notation following the method declaration, = 0, tells us that the method is purely virtual and therefore that the class is abstract.

65

All of this allows us another mechanism for abstracting classes into simple pieces of code which are easy to follow, and easy to implement. A listNode would look similar to *Listing 5.2*.

```
C++ Declaration:
    class listNode
    {
    protected:
        listNode * next;
    public:
        listNode();
        ~listNode();
        listNode * next();          // Get the next node in the list
        void    next( listNode *);  // Set the next node in the list
        virtual void process() = 0;
    };

Object Pascal Declaration:
        listNode = Object
            next : ^listNode;

    Constructor Init;
    Destructor  Done;
    Procedure  SetNext( node: ^listNode);
    Function    GetNext : ^listNode;
    Procedure Process; virtual;
    End;
```

Listing 5.2

That's all. When you want to create a list of something, you derive what you want in the list at some point from listNode, and implement process according to how you want to process that particular class, or classes as the case may be. *Listing 5.3* shows how the list class would look.

C++ Declaration:
```
class List
{
protected:
    ListNode * head;          // head node of list
    ListNode * current;       // pointer to current node in list
public:
    List();                   // constructor
    ~List();                  // destructor
    void        head(ListNode *);
    void        current(ListNode *);
    ListNode *  head();
    ListNode *  current();
    ListNode *  next();
};
```

OOPascal Declaration:
```
list = Object
    Head : ^listNode;
    Current : ^listNode;

    Constructor  Init;
    Destructor   Done;
    Procedure    SetHead( node: ^listNode);
    Procedure    SetCurrent( node: ^listNode);
    Function     GetHead : ^listNode;
    Function     GetCurrent : ^listNode;
    Function     GetNext : ^listNode;
End;
```

Listing 5.3

A list must be attached to something in order to be accessed later, so the head data member provides the link between the list and the actual nodes in the list. The current data member allows for us to know where we currently are in the list. The standard accessor methods do exactly as previously described, setting and retrieving the values of their corresponding data members.

The next method, however, is a little different. It will set the current pointer to be the next node in the list, and return that pointer to you. But there is no next data member in the class, it is in the ListNode class. So the method must call upon the current ListNode to return the ListNode stored in its next data member, and use that to set the current data member. It might look like *Listing 5.4.*

C++ Definition:

```
ListNode * List::next()
{
      current = current->next();     // set current to next node in list
      return current;
};
```

Object Pascal Definition:

```
Function list.GetNext : ^listNode;
   Begin
      Current := Current^.GetNext;
      GetNext := Current
   End;
```

Listing 5.4

The code for a List and a ListNode is quite simplistic when it is abstracted using object-oriented techniques. This simplification makes maintenance over long periods of time easier and makes more sense than the procedural approach of sending a list to a function and having to worry about typecasting or data typing.

Another advantage of abstraction involves provability and testing. After creating a class, it needs to be tested to insure that it does what was specified in the design. A thorough test of the class can be done by testing each method to insure that it works correctly. Even the accessors should be tested.

It may seem like it shouldn't be important to test code that simply returns a variable to you, but it is necessary. Making the assumption that an accessor always "just returns a variable" to you can be a dangerous thought.

Depending on the level of encapsulation involved in the class, a simple accessor method might turn out to be a complicated binary search through several layers of the accessor methods of other classes! Therefore, all accessors should be tested to insure that they do return the object or value that you expect. Debuggers can aid you in testing a class, because you can walk through the code and examine the class at each step, making sure that the data is being manipulated the way that you expect it to be manipulated and the way that is specified in the design.

When a class is thoroughly tested and found to be a sound class, the code involved is unlikely to be wrong at a later date. Its interaction with other classes may change, forcing the developer to examine the class and its implementation again. As the system and subsequent applications grow, you will spend less time in finished classes because they have already been proven to be reliable and correct.

Templates as Abstraction

C++ uses a *template* in many cases to facilitate data abstraction. You can think of a template as a pattern that is used to construct common classes that hold different types of data. It is most commonly used with the common abstract data types: arrays, queues, stacks and trees.

An extremely common template is one built for a dynamic array, which is an array that continually grows in size as you index into it. *Listing 5.5* contains the definition of a simple dynamic array template.

```
#ifndef DARRAY_H                    // used to aviod multiple compilation.
#define DARRAY_H

const int ReSize = 1;               // we allocate one new element at a time.

template <class Type>
class Array
{
protected:                          // things available only to child classes.
    int reSize(int);                // re-allocates the data array.
    int size;
    int sizeChange;                 // size to re-allocate.
    Type *data;                     // type is replaced at compile time with
                                    // class name.
public:
    Array(int = 0,int = ReSize);    // default constructor.
    Array(const Array&);            // copy constructor, used to copy another
                                    // array.
    ~Array();                       // destructor.
    Type& operator [](int);         // accessor for any 1 element of the array.
    Array operator = (const Array&); // assignment operator.
    int Size()const {return size;}  // gets the current size of the array.
};

template <class Type>
Array<Type>::Array(int newSize, int delta)
{
    size = newSize;                 // set the size to whatever the instantiator
                                    // said.
    sizeChange = delta;             // save the amount to grow by in delta.
        if (newSize > 0)
            data = new Type [size]; // allocate space for size elements.
        else
            data = NULL;
}

template <class Type>
Array<Type>::Array(const Array<Type> &x)
{
    size = x.size;                  // copy all fields of x.
```

```
        sizeChange = x.sizeChange;
        data = new Type[size];          // but use our own storage space,
                                        // so when x is destroyed, we're still valid.
        for (int i = 0; i < size; I++)  // copy each element of x into our array.
            data[i] = x.data[i];        // note that we will use x's equals
                                        //  operator, if over-ridden.
}
```

```
template <class Type>
Array<Type> Array<Type>::operator = (const Array<Type> &x)
{
    if (this != &x) {                   // if they're already the same, do nothing.
        if (data) delete [] data;       // otherwise, copy each feild of x into our
                                        // fields.
        size = x.size;
        sizeChange = x.sizeChange;
        data = new Type[size];
        for (int i = 0; i < size; i++)
            data[i] = x.data[i];
    }
    return *this;                       // return ourself, so if there are chained
                                        // assignments, they come out correctly
}
```

```
template <class Type>
Array<Type>::~Array()
{
        if (data) delete [] data;       // deallocate our data space.
}
```

```
template <class Type>
Type& Array<Type>::operator [] (int i)
{
        static Type errorDump;

        if (i < 0)                      // if the index is negative, set error.
            return errorDump;
        if (i >= size)                  // same if index is too big.
            reSize(i);
        return data[i];                 // if everythings okay, return the element
                                        // requested.
    }
```

```
template <class Type>
int Array<Type>::reSize(int i)
{
    int increase = ((i - size)/sizeChange + 1)*sizeChange;
                            // calculate the amount to increase by.
    int tsize = size + increase;
    Type *temp = new Type [tsize];
                            // allocate enough space for the
                            // whole array.
    if (data)               // if there's data, copy it.
        for (int j = 0; j < size; j++)
            temp[j] = data[j];
                if (data)           // and delete it.
                    delete [] data;
                data = temp;
                size = tsize;       // reset size.
                return 1;
}
#endif
```

Listing 5.5

When you declare a dynamic array of some type, say an array of PERSON, you do so as follows:

```
Array<PERSON>    personArray;
```

You access the array as you would a normal array, using [x] to index it, where x is some integer indicating the index of the object in the array you want returned to you. The only behavioral difference between a dynamic array and a normal array is if you reference an index that is out of bounds, the array will grow to a size that allows you to access that index.

What happens with this template is where <class Type> occurs the preprocessor replaces it with the declared classes and generates code for a brand-new class, in this case a person array. This is an even stronger example of not only abstraction but also of encapsulation.

You never see the generated code for the class, or know anything about how it is working other than the knowledge you have of how the template works. This level of abstraction and encapsulation is an added benefit. And, you can use it with any type you define, because it is only a template and not a true class until it is compiled.

While a template gives you a large amount of flexibility and reuse of code, it creates new object code for each template you declare, because the compiler must resolve the <type>s within the template and generate a class for each one, even if you are declaring two or more templates that use the same <type>. This will cause larger executable sizes, and possibly poorer performance overall. It is often times a better choice to simply create an abstract base class that uses void pointers as its data members, and typecast in your source code. Templates are certainly easier and safer than void pointers and typecasting, but size is often an important factor in an application, especially if it is commercial. Consider the advantages and disadvantages, and make your choices early on. It becomes more difficult to throw away code that has been implemented and tested as the deadlines draw nearer.

CHAPTER 6
Miscellaneous Subjects

On the road to object land, you must wonder not only about the paradigm and its intricacies, but about the differences in the languages. Discussing languages, especially object-oriented ones, with most programmers, can be extremely frustrating, because they tend to choose one particular language and proclaim it as the only language to use—even if they have no experience with any of the other languages.

Here, we will discuss some of the fundamental differences between the three languages we have chosen to use for this book: Borland's Turbo Pascal with Objects, Digitalk's Smalltalk/V and Borland's C++ 3.1. We will offer both the advantages and disadvantages of each language, including estimations of what types of systems are best implemented in each language. Every language has its particular niche in the world, and object-oriented languages are no exception.

Identity vs. Equality

Identity and *equality* are two very different things. Identity means two things are the same object; equality means the two things have the same value.

Identity is most often performed on pointers, or addresses, to determine whether the instances they point to are indeed the same object under different aliases, or if they are not the same. If the addresses of both instances are the same, it is said to be identical.

Equality means that the two instances contain the same data. Equality is not automatically implemented for you in C++ or Borland's Turbo Pascal with Objects. It is Smalltalk/V.

Identity is determined by comparing two instances using the == method, and equality by using the = method. In C++, equality and identity initially use the == operator. You can overload this operator within your own classes to determine equality based on a single attribute or a set of attributes. For example, in the class PERSON you might say that two people are equal if their hairColor is the same. You would overload the == operator as follows:

pseudo-code:

```
BOOL operator == (PERSON & aPerson)
    if this object's hairColor is the same as aPerson's hairColor return TRUE
    else return FALSE
```

actual code:

```
BOOL operator == (PERSON &aPerson)
{
    return (BOOL) hairColor == aPerson hairColor;
};
```

Note: BOOL is not really a data type in C or C++, but it is generally accepted and standard to typedef a BOOL to be a short (or int) and #define TRUE 1 and FALSE 0. This method returns TRUE if the hairColor of both people is the same, and FALSE if they are not.

You can overload this operator to check on any data member, or even the time of day if you wish. You can overload the = method in Smalltalk/V to achieve the same results, if you so desire.

In Borland's Turbo Pascal with Objects it is necessary to implement an equals method in your classes if you desire to check equality. There is no corresponding overloading of operators that allow you a quick and easy access to an operator.

However, identity and equality are easily confused, and forcing you to implement such a method insures that you will not confuse the two, and that the comparison you truly want is the comparison you really get.

Language Comparison: Syntactical Differences

One of the biggest differences in the three languages we have chosen to use is in the *instantiation* of objects, or the creation of instances. Each language uses a special method called a constructor, but their uses vary so greatly that they can confuse a developer moving from one language to the next.

In Smalltalk and Borland's Turbo Pascal with Objects, the constructor is really a specialized method. Both Smalltalk and Borland's Turbo Pascal with Objects allow for the constructor to be named at the developer's discretion. Almost all class methods in Smalltalk are constructors, in the literal sense that they return to the caller an instantiated object.

In C++, the constructors must follow a specific naming convention, that being that they are named the same as the class name. Constructors and destructors in Borland's Turbo Pascal with Objects are similar to their constructors in that they can be named any thing the developer wants, although academic convention is to name them Init and Done, respectively.

C++ uses a tilde (~) in front of the class' name to indicate a destructor (note that in C, the tilde character is the NOT operator, meaning NOT classname), and Smalltalk has no explicit destructors, because its extensive garbage collection routines handle the deallocation of memory behind the scenes.

The allocation of memory is done explicitly in C++ and Borland's Turbo Pascal with Objects. Even here there are subtle syntactic differences, however, since in C++ the allocation method is an operator, and in Borland's Turbo Pascal with Objects the method is an actual global method. In C++, dynamic memory is allocated using the new operator. Because it is an operator, it can be over-ridden at the class level in order to enhance debugging, or to institute exception handling. Borland's Turbo Pascal with Objects does not have this feature. Smalltalk handles memory allocation on a much lower level than the developer.

Unless you are interfacing with DynamicLinkLibraries (DLLs) you will rarely find the need to actually allocate memory in the conventional way. You still allocate, just on a very abstract level. All derivatives of Object (that is to say all classes in Smalltalk save one), inherit the class method called new, which allocates the memory necessary for the class and returns a new instance of the class to the caller. You can override this method in your own class, which allows for things such as initialization of instance variables, before returning an instance to the caller.

The Purist Language

The biggest difference between the languages is that Smalltalk is a pure object-oriented environment, and C++ and Borland's Turbo Pascal with Objects are not. This means that there are certain pieces of C++ and Pascal that are bound to traditional C and Pascal, such as operators and base data types.

In C++ and Pascal, you cannot modify the behavior of a base data type, such as a float or a character. They are endemic to the system and cannot be changed by the developer. In addition, in Smalltalk all methods must have a receiver, or a calling class. In Smalltalk, the statement 1 + 2 is by no means a simple arithmetic computation of two base data types. 1 is an object, 2 is an object, and + is a method. 1 is the receiver, by virtue of being on the left-hand side of the statement.

The method probably looks something like this in actual Smalltalk code:

```
+ anInteger
    ^self + anInteger
```

Integers, strings and characters have special literal meaning in Smalltalk; they are interpreted immediately into the correct instance of a given class, such as Integer or Character. The integers 0 to 9 are global instances of the class Integer. They are instantiated upon startup of the system. Then are they allowed to send and receive messages to and from other objects.

This is perhaps the hardest thing for new developers in Smalltalk to grasp—everything in Smalltalk is either a message (method) or an object. Period. There are no exceptions. Even nil, more commonly known in C++ as NULL and in Borland's Turbo Pascal with Objects also as nil, is an object.

While instance variables in Smalltalk are merely pointers to objects, they are still representative of objects, and must be thought of in that light in order for the developer to properly handle the environment. So while in C++ and Borland's Turbo Pascal with Objects, 1 + 1 will always give you 2 (if it does not there is something terribly wrong with your compiler), in Smalltalk this can be changed to suit the needs of the developer.

While it is inadvisable for developers to change the base behavior of any class in the class library distributed with Smalltalk, it is not impossible, and in many cases enhancements to the base data types are often desirable.

Situational Mathematics

In C++ and Borland's Turbo Pascal with Objects, if you evaluate 1 + 2 * 3, the answer is 7, every time. C++ and Borland's Turbo Pascal with Objects follow standard mathematical operator precedence when evaluating computational statements involving base mathematical types.

Smalltalk, however, does not. Smalltalk evaluates strictly from left to right, regardless of operator precedence. This could be because + and * are not actually operators, but are instead messages being sent to each object as it is evaluated. 1 + 2 is evaluated, and the resulting object is then sent the message * 3, which evaluates to the object 9.

This is what we refer to as situational mathematics: When you're in Smalltalk, math acts differently than people would expect. Smalltalk is not the language of choice when dealing with heavy mathematical computations anyway, but even for simple computations it is important to remember the manner in which Smalltalk handles operators.

You can force evaluation of any methods in the order you desire by simply surrounding them with parentheses. 1 + (2 * 3) will evaluate to 7 in Smalltalk, just as you would expect. But this illustration reiterates the most basic fact of Smalltalk: everything is an object and you send messages to those objects.

Choosing Your Language

Smalltalk is a very good language if you are in a situation where your company can afford to shell out unlimited funds on hardware, and execution speed is not critical to the success and/or acceptance of the final product. Smalltalk is consistently slower than either C++ or Object Pascal, given the same application. The size of the binary (executable) created by Smalltalk is also usually larger than the equivalent C++ or Turbo Pascal with Objects system.

Smalltalk falls further behind the other languages if you are executing many floating point calculations or file Input/Output (I/O). File I/O is slowed because there are no built-in classes or operators for binary data files. Aside from performance issues, this means that everything you save to disk in Smalltalk is accessible with a text editor. You need to consider this if you want your data to be secure. All of the other shortcomings are the price you pay for the major benefit of Smalltalk — abstraction.

The further you move away from the hardware and operating system of your machine, the more your performance degrades. While careful coding can minimize the effect of this abstraction, it has been our experience that Smalltalk programmers don't overly concern themselves with speed issues (even Smalltalk programmers that do concern themselves with speed in other languages).

The last shortcoming of Smalltalk is an offshoot of the distance from the hardware and operating system at which the programmer operates: There are some things that are nearly impossible to do in Smalltalk (in particular, operating system and hardware specific tasks).

On a positive note, Smalltalk relieves the designers and programmers from having to concern themselves with basic data structures. While the other languages attempt to do this to some extent, none of them comes close to the features built into Smalltalk. Because of Smalltalk's complete library of container classes, the developers can concentrate on the problem at hand, rather than how to implement linked lists, dynamic arrays, etc.

Smalltalk also gains a plus for its weak typing. In the structured world, strong typing was considered almost essential to successful software development, but in an integrated, object-oriented environment, good documentation of code replaces strong typing, and exploits the strengths of polymorphism to a greater extent.

Probably the most subtle, but most useful advantage to Smalltalk is that it is interpreted. At run time, you can create code based on the current environment, and execute that code. Smalltalk's other advantages include advanced exception handling and automated memory management. Smalltalk is currently implemented for DOS, Windows, Windows NT, OS/2 and X-Windows.

C++'s primary advantage over the other languages is the number of commercially available class libraries, tools, books and development environments. Another big plus is the number of platforms for which C++ compilers have been implemented. You can find C++ compilers for almost any modern computer system, aiding in portability immensely.

One of C++'s strengths is also a major weakness. C++ inherited strong type checking from C. While this means that a poor comment will never leave you wondering what type a variable holds, it also means that whenever you take advantage of inheritance, you must "cast" (tell the compiler which type to use) the variable to the type you really are using.

Of all the languages discussed here, C++ is (usually) the fastest. Your choice of class libraries will affect your performance and binary file size drastically. So if you are using C++ for its speed and size, be careful of your choices for class libraries. Primary among C++'s weaknesses is that like C, it is cryptic. While C++ is a vast improvement over its predecessor in this respect, it still can throw new object-oriented programmers for a loop.

Development time for C++ is the highest of the three languages, because you have more control over the lower levels of your machine and operating system. Again, class libraries can dramatically improve the development time for a C++ project, but cannot make it as short as the same project would be in Smalltalk.

Turbo Pascal with Objects is an extension of Pascal. Perhaps the biggest of Turbo Pascal with Objects's advantages is that its learning curve is much lower than either of the other object-oriented languages. This is because the extensions provided to allow object-oriented programming on top of Pascal are few. You cannot truly encapsulate data, in the sense of protecting data from outside access, in this language. With proper design, this disadvantage can become negligible, but it is a concern.

Turbo Pascal with Objects, like C, C++ and Pascal is strongly typed, which lends itself well to more maintainable code than Smalltalk. Turbo Pascal with Objects is available for DOS and Microsoft Windows, although there are a limited number of class libraries for the language.

Turbo Pascal with Objects is heavily used in academia along with Pascal, mainly because of its learning curve. It is more difficult to blow up a Pascal or Turbo Pascal with Objects application than it is to do with its counterparts of C and C++. This is mainly because it is more difficult to manipulate pointers and memory, and the available options for doing so are more limited.

Part Two

Analysis and Design of Object-Oriented Systems

CHAPTER 7
Analysis, Design and Modeling

In object-oriented development, a large portion of your team's time will be spent in the analysis and design phase. While the estimates of development ratios vary by the author, it seems generally accepted that you will spend more time in analysis and design of your project than you will coding. This is, all things considered, good news for the software industry.

Problems that are thoroughly analyzed, and coding that has been well designed makes a much sounder and better accepted product than one that is created by hacking at the code throughout the project. It has however, caused a bewildering number of object-oriented analysis and design methodologies to appear. We have found that many of these methodologies fall apart when used in a real-life situation, or when used to implement particularly large and/or complex systems.

Approach to Analysis and Design

We do not subscribe to any of the popular analysis (OOA) and design (OOD) techniques currently in use in the object paradigm. While we are familiar with many of them, we also feel that most of the OOA/OOD techniques available place too much emphasis upon notation and not enough on the technique and solving of real-world problems.

Each of us has read, or at least attempted to read, books on the major methodologies and have put the book down because it relied too heavily on a notation which was, when it came time for real-world use, unreasonable. For this reason, we have chosen to stick with very simple notations, as with those used in the first half of this book, and with simple documents for analysis and design that we have found to be useful for real-world projects.

Because we have used them for both commercial and in-house applications, we know them to be usable and constructive, something many other methodologies lack. Other techniques, when ignoring the fact that they do work and are completely correct, are simply too complex and wrapped up in the methodology to be of much use to those who must do the job every day.

We must point out that it would be worth any developer's time to explore the methodologies available, and evaluate them in light of the needs of their departments or even on a project-by-project basis. Most developers, unless forced to change, seem to choose one methodology and stick with it throughout their careers. But the rapid pace at which our field changes does not allow for this kind of stick-in-the-mud attitude. You may not find a methodology that feels comfortable for you. If this is true for you, you may want to experiment and pull together pieces of methodologies or create your own. There is not one best methodology, and you must decide what works best for your company, your developers and your projects. We have long argued about the best available methodology, but when it comes time to actually start a project, we both inevitably turn to the simple system described next.

Waterfall vs. Spiral

Most of the methodologies available today are based on either the *waterfall* approach to software design, or on the iterative *spiral* approach. Before we dive into an example of designing a system using object-oriented analysis and design, we want to make sure that you understand the difference between these two approaches.

The waterfall approach to software development is based on the idea that development should be done in steps (i.e., analysis, design, code, test), with each step as complete as possible before the next step is started. When the complete series of steps is complete, the whole series is repeated, in view of the current state of the system, and new information that has become available since the original design was completed.

The spiral approach to software design treats software development as a much smaller circle, where only enough analysis is done to move on to the design phase. Then, the other steps are completed in order, and the whole system is started again, taking analysis to the next level, based on knowledge gained in the last iteration.

The two systems sound very similar, but in practice produce much varied results. Our experience has been that systems that use the waterfall approach are much more sound than those that are developed using the Spiral approach. This is a predictable result because waterfall attempts to address as many potential problem areas as possible before coding begins. And, developer's often loathe throwing away or even radically changing code they already have written even if it can be proven that the change or removal will be a benefit to the system overall.

In both cases, analysis consists of determining the objects necessary and their respected relationships. Design consists of further specifying the objects' attributes, methods and inter-relationships with other objects. The design phase takes you right into actual coding, and should be complete enough to allow the coder to know what the designer wants the object to be, how it should act, and how it should communicate with other objects. This, without being so constraining as to give the coder option on how the actual implementation should be handled.

For example, design should not entail the naming of parameters, or (usually) algorithms to be used, or any other such level of detail. Those who are coding take little joy in their work if they are handed a design document with the coding practically finished because then they are doing little more than data entry. You should get to know the developers who will be coding from your design, and attempt to learn the nuances of their coding style, and what they need from a design. Keep it simple, yet detailed enough to let the coder know what is expected without writing the code for him.

A good rule of thumb for what each step of the design process should entail is: "Analysis is *what* we need to do the job, design is *how* we're going to do the job, coding is actually *doing* the job, and testing is *proving* that we did the job correctly."

In the following sections, we will walk through the analysis and design of a simple business, illustrating the use of simple notations and documentation to aid in the process. Our approach is technically a waterfall approach. Having developed applications using both a waterfall and a spiral approach, we find that the waterfall approach is more complete and tends to create less complex applications than its counterpart. For that reason we use a more direct line when considering the overall project. Within analysis, and later on design, we will use a spiral approach in order to complete the phase, as a straight shot is unlikely to create a workable model.

However, each phase should be as complete as possible before moving on to the next phase. So we begin with the analysis of the business.

Business Analysis of The Caterer's

The Caterer's, as we will call them, is a small independent catering business. It employs less than 10 employees, and services a relatively small town. Customers usually phone in their orders to one of the employees, and pay either in one lump sum or in payments, if the order is extremely large. The Caterer's needs a system which will track customer's orders and payments, keep track of the inventory, employee's pay, and inform the business when an order is necessary for inventory items.

This, in a nutshell, is what we will be using for our discussions on analysis and design. Business analysis and its requirements are the first step in any development effort. Some companies have a staff that writes these requirements for internal or external users, and then they coordinate with the development team to insure that the application is meeting those requirements. Other companies require that the development staff, or part of the staff, engage in this process themselves.

In many ways, getting the development staff involved in the business process or requirements aspects of the development process can be an effective decision because it allows the developers to more fully understand what it is they will be developing, and how the users will need to apply the program. However, not every developer is a requirements writer, and not every developer can be a great analyst of business processes. Therefore, it is essential that this part of the analysis is reviewed and is acceptable to those whose job it is to finalize these requirements.

Usually, the people who will make good requirements writers and analysts are obvious. Someone who has a large store of relevant business knowledge, will likely be successful at requirements writing, and an individual who consistently suggests solutions to rough problems is an ideal candidate for analysts positions. Because both of these jobs have a tendency to keep a developer from doing very much coding, make sure that this is acceptable to them.

When the business analysis or requirements are completed, the process of analysis from a development standpoint can begin.

There are many schools of thought on object analysis and on determining what the major classes in any given system should be, and most center around the nouns of a system. Where do those nouns come from? It's an easier task with a requirements document, but even then the process of laying out the objects in a system can be quite tedious. Walking through an application, from a user's perspective, can offer some insight into determining what the objects are.

For example, if we were to walk through a simple scenario of this order entry system, we might be able to begin our analysis.

1. *Customer calls the business*
      Customer, Business
2. *Customer places an order with an employee*
      Order, Employee
3. *Business prepares the order*
4. *Customers pays for the order*

So far we have a customer, a business, an order, and an employee. There seems to be a lot more going on in each of these scenarios, so we need to ask some questions:

1. *How does a customer place an order?*
2. *How does a customer pay for an order?*
3. *How is the order recorded by the employee?*
4. *How is the customer's payment recorded?*

Questions 1 and 3, and 2 and 4 seem to go together, that is if we can answer how an order is placed we would probably have the answer to how the order is recorded. The same can be said of the customer's payment for an order. So we ask question 1.

The customer calls up and talks to an employee,
placing an order for a dinner she is planning.
The employee records the order on an order form
of some sort, itemizing it, and then arriving at a
total cost which the customer will pay.

This business process will create an order form, and will place within that form items. That gives us two more objects: Form and Item. If we ask question 2, we may find even more objects.

The customer receives a bill, and sends in a check to pay for
all or part of the order which has been received of the company.

We have a Bill, and a Payment object from this question's answer, or do we? It certainly looks that way from the answer to the question, and our initial instinct is to say there are at least two objects in the answer. We'll leave it as such for now, and see what happens as our analysis continues to move forward. So far, we have discovered the following objects.

Customer
Business
Employee
Order
Form
Item
Bill
Payment

Let's work with these for the time being and see where it leads us.

The End User Approach

We could have approached this from another, just as valid, point of view. When considering the application we are developing, what is it we want the user to be able to do? In other words, instead of looking at what the business process is from a step-by-step analysis, look at what the application should allow a user to do. At some point, someone has to have sat down and said, 'We have decided that we need an application that does X, Y and Z, and allows our employees to do K.' This method allows us to not only do initial analysis, it also makes clear what the users expect from a new system, and what is involved in it. It might be a good idea to sit down with the end users and ask them what they expect from the system. From this we can garnish quite a bit of information about the objects in the system.

The Caterer's have decided to computerize its system, and have brought a team in to write this new system for the company. Before the development team can do anything, they must understand what it is that the business management wants out of the new application.

Sitting down with the management, and later on with the users of the system, will give the development effort extra synergy in the area of not only creating a well thought out and solid application, but in acceptance of the application by the users. After all, a system that is well designed and implemented is a beautiful thing, but if the users do not accept and use it, the development process has been wasted, as well as quite a bit of time, effort and money.

With this in mind, the development team and the business sit down, and the business lists off the following needs for their application:

> storage of customer information, including orders and payments
> storage of employee information, including pay
> ability to print customer bills
> ability to print orders for inventory items

With these needs in mind, we can find most of the same objects we discovered using the first technique. We see customers, orders, payments, employees and items. What we don't see here is, what is the customer information, what is an order, what is involved in a payment? Yet because we now know what the application should do when finished, we can ask these questions of The Caterer's and come up with the same set of classes, data and manipulation methods that we arrived at with our first technique.

There are many other ways to approach the initial analysis of a project. In many cases, development teams are simply handed documents that contain a paper prototype of what the application looks like—down to every dialog and screen detailed out for them—and a description of what each screen or dialog allows the user to do. Along with this, there is often times miscellaneous information about security, hardware requirements, and application management issues.

If this is the case, the developers involved in the initial analysis need to read the user requirements document thoroughly, and walk through it, looking for the major objects of the system. Most of them will be obvious, but some will remain hidden throughout the first, second and even third passes through the document. Often times, iterative analysis is necessary, including meetings with those who wrote the document in order to insure that what the analysts understand about the application are in synch with the intent of the document's writers.

If there aren't user requirements, or requirements about the layout or look of the application, a prototype may be in order to insure that the look and feel of the application is what the business needs and wants. The job of the development staff is not only to provide a solid usable application, but to insure that it meets the needs of the users, and that the application is acceptable to those who must work with it every day.

A prototype, which generally involves only the graphical user interface (GUI), could easily be designed after the next step in analysis, which is determining what the actual meat of all the classes are, in other words, what data they hold.

Defining Data Members

The next step in analysis is to describe each of these objects in terms of the data they are responsible for in the system. Some might argue that this is not part of the analysis phase, but is instead part of the design stage. We would argue that in order to design a system, you must first know what objects are in the system. An object is not simply a word, but is defined by the data responsibilities it holds. Therefore it is important to determine what data is held by what object in the analysis stage in order to better determine what each object will be doing to the data, and how they will interact, in the design stage.

In addition, it is during the analysis phase that objects are discovered, and often times subsequently dismissed as either unnecessary objects, or as data members of some other yet undiscovered object. Many objects can be grouped, or classed together under a common base class. You can only discover this fact during the determination of data member responsibility. To leave this process until the design phase is to court disaster.

It is normal for developers to become more attached to objects as they move through the phases of development, and it becomes more and more difficult as you move forward to dismiss objects, create new objects, and classify objects into groups. Systems grow in complexity most often because of a change to the analysis and decisions made about objects in later phases, because much of the design, and sometimes code, is already in place and it is difficult for any developer to simply throw the code or design away and begin anew.

For these reasons, it is imperative to lay out your system as completely as possible during the analysis phase, and change it as little as possible in later stages.

The first object we identified was a Customer. A customer generally has a name, an address, a phone number, and some unique identifier (usually a number of some kind). Customers place orders, so we will give the customer a list of orders. A customer also makes payments, and therefore needs to keep a list of payments.

Notice that although we are making decisions about the data for which a customer is responsible, that we are not deciding on what each data member's type will be, such as an integer, a float, or a string. These are decisions that are best left for the design phase.

At this point, we may not have even decided on a language yet. The analysis should be as generic toward languages as possible, and should, if possible, be done in such a way as to allow non-developers to understand the overall system. This will help when it comes time to include the users or requirements writers in analysis sessions, and when the analysis is reviewed to insure that the application will meet the user's needs and wants. An Order would contain a list of items ordered and a balance due. Because an order keeps track of the balance due, it should probably also keep track of payments made on itself, so it can keep a list of payments also.

If we continue with this train of thought, we might come up with a list of classes and data responsibilities as follows:

Customer
  Identification, name, address, phone, orders, payments
Order
  Items, payments, total cost
Employee
  Identification, name, address, phone, pay received
Business
  Customers, employees, orders, payments, items
Item
  Number in stock, order level, price to customer, cost to business

You will notice that we are missing something, namely the Bill object we picked out earlier. What would a bill be responsible for knowing? It would know its customer, the order number, and the balance due. Surprisingly enough, each customer contains a list of orders, each that know its balance due. It would be inefficient to store this information again in another object. Instead, a Bill will most likely become a method within Customer that would print out the customer's information, list of orders that have balances due, and a total balance due for the customer.

We notice several things when we look over this list of objects. The most glaring thing we see is that both Customer and Employee have several of the same data members. These two are prime candidates for grouping. We'll create another class, Person, and move those common data responsibilities up to Person, leaving only the different data to the two classes. We now have:

Person
Identification, name, address, phone
Customer
Orders, payments
Employee
Pay received

While it does not appear that we have accomplished much with this move, we have done two significant things:

Created an abstract, reusable class in Person.
Reduced the redundancy involved in implementation of the two classes by placing the common data, and therefore accessor methods, in one place.

We also notice that the Item class has a data member that tells us that when an item in stock gets to a certain level, we need to reorder it. This tells us that the business must also place orders, something we had not previously considered. In order to rectify this, we need to add it to the Business class. But we already have a data member for orders from customers. How will we keep the two separate? Perhaps this is just a matter of semantics, and we can simply call the list something else, such as invoices. For now, we will do just that. So now our Business class looks like this:

Business
Customers, employees, orders, payments, items, invoices

Invoices and orders are a lot alike, in fact the only difference we can see right now is that one is essentially money the business takes in, and one represents money the business gives out. In addition to this, an employee receives pay (an outlay for the company) and the customer sends in payments (take in for the company). Because they all involve amounts of money, perhaps we can abstract a class from these entities that deals with money, and then create subclasses for these other classes from those entities. Of course, the only difference between the two entities would be whether money is coming in to the business or going out.

This difference is indicative of data manipulation, and does not require additional or different data. For that reason, we can create a single class, we will call it Transaction, whose data responsibility is an amount of money. Order, invoice, payment, and employeePay will be subclasses of Transaction, and will manipulate that amount of money differently according to the type of class it is.

We have begun to create a class hierarchy, and at this point it would be a good idea to see it visually (*Figure 7.1*):

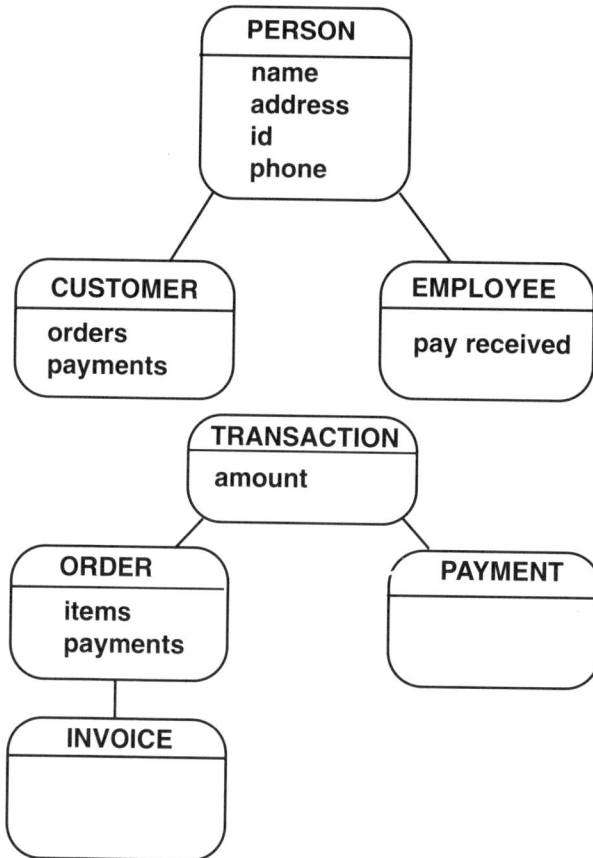

Figure 7.1 : Class Hierarchy.

The other classes: Item and Business, have no superclasses and no subclasses. While it is far from a complex system, it does simplify the understanding of the analysis so far to see the hierarchy visually. It is easy enough to write down, but within the object paradigm it is much clearer and easier to view the hierarchies as they grow more complex. What we have done in a broad sense, is analysis in a straight line.

However, you will notice that we defined several classes, and then changed them later on in the process. This is not such a straight forward approach. In fact, we may change them yet again in the analysis stage, after consulting with the business process experts, users, or requirements writers. This is what we meant earlier when we said that while we use an overall waterfall approach to object analysis and design, that within each phase we approach the process in a spiral, or iterative, manner. A combination of these two approaches seems to allow the development process the flexibility it needs with this paradigm, and at the same time constrains it from becoming a complex monster in the end.

Application Prototyping

Now that we have determined what the data members of the classes are, we can move into prototyping. Prototyping is generally an empty shell, an exercise in making sure that the look and feel of the application is in accordance with the user's wants and needs. It also can be a good tool for insuring that the development staff has interpreted the information garnered from meetings with the business and/or users correctly. In most languages, especially those whose basis is the Microsoft Windows operating system, phototyping can be a simple task. Many tools, such as Borland's Resource Workshop, Microsoft's App Studio, and Object Share International's WindowBuilderPro for Smalltalk/V can be helpful during prototyping.

All of the aforementioned tools allow the developer to design windows, dialogs and menus, allowing the developer to get a feel for how the application flows. If the developers create a prototype, be sure to include the users in reviews of the prototype. They can provide information critical to the success of the application by pointing out why the application makes some part of their job more difficult or easier.

Perhaps the developers have incorrectly interpreted some information about the application and how it should work. If this is the case, it might be caught in the prototype and allows for the developers to correct this problem before design has begun and before any code has actually been written. Prototyping is optional, however it is always exciting for the users, management or other requesting departments to get an idea of what they will be getting in the end. It can also help to bring departments closer together and help to turn out a better product than might have otherwise been produced.

Note though, that it is generally a bad idea to prototype a project, then attempt to use your prototype code in the final system. Prototyping code is usually "throw-away," written without the benefit of a complete analysis and design. The cases we have seen where the developers have tried to use prototype code to save development time have spent more than they save.

The Design Phase

Now that we have decided on the objects that will be present in our system, and their data responsibilities, we need to move into the design phase and determine a great deal more important information about each class, such as each class' manipulation responsibilities, the interaction between classes, and common protocols for classes.

We also need to determine what the data types for each class will be, and how will a given class reference some other class. We have several classes that store lists of other classes within them. We need to examine them closely and determine whether storing actual instances of the other class is best, or whether storing some unique identifier that identifies the other entity is in order.

These types of questions and ultimately their decisions will affect the complexity, performance, and size of the application in the end. These are not trivial issues we are dealing with, since hardware limitations, operating system limitations, and general acceptance of performance by users are all necessary to the overall success of the development effort.

Data typing often will be determined by the language in which you are working. Consider the identification data member of the class Person. A large business, which expects to be storing less than 250 customers and employees, should consider this data member differently than one which expects to be storing less than 4.2 billion employees and customers. The differences are subtle, and are calculated in bits, but they are there.

In C++ and Turbo Pascal with Objects, an identifier for a person, for a business storing less than 250 total people, should seriously consider storing that value as an unsigned character, which is stored as only 8 bits (1 byte).

Normally, you might simply store this as an integer. This is not so terrible, but because an integer is 16 bits (2 bytes), for 200 people you are wasting a total of 200 bytes.

Many might ignore this small amount, but what about the differences between an integer and a long? An unsigned integer ranges from 0 to 65535, and an unsigned long from 0 to 4,294,967,295 with the former being two bytes and the latter being four. Assuming that the application stored on average 60,000 customers, the difference between the two is now 120,000 bytes. And this is only one data member. Spread these types of differences out over several data members and you are wasting not only memory, but ultimately disk space.

So consider your choice of data types seriously, a bad choice can degrade performance and cause storage problems over time, neither of which makes for a successful application.

Those developing in Smalltalk might ignore this issue altogether, because all data members, regardless of how they are intended to be used, are stored in memory, as pointers, which is 4 bytes, period. However, even these developers must face the fact that their data must be stored somewhere on disk or tape or some other medium, and that the larger the object they are pointing to, the more storage space will be required, and the performance when loading or saving such objects will seriously degrade if multiple objects are stored within a single class.

The largest problem with the object-oriented paradigm is back referencing, and is addressed in depth in *Chapter 8*.

Consider it carefully, it is an important part of object technology and is critical to the success of your application.

With this in mind, we have decided to store the identification number as an unsigned integer for C++, in Turbo Pascal with Objects, and a LargePositiveInteger in Smalltalk. Name will be stored as a string

(Note: We don't have much of a choice here, but we do have control over the size of the string! We can limit the string to a standard size, or dynamically allocate it to the exact size needed at run time. We must remember, however, that by doing this, storage may be a more complex issue than if we were to use objects of differing sizes in the same field. Writing out is not a large problem, but reading back in can become quite a chore).

The phone number can be stored as a 10 character string, or 13 characters if you want to store the parentheses and hyphens. That is a matter of formatting and style, but we would argue that for storage purposes we should store the number as a compact string and simply format it for display or printing later.

The orders and payments, which are lists of their respective objects, could be stored as any one of several abstract data types (ADT). There are lists, arrays or trees, and many different types of each of these data types. We can say for sure that whichever data type we choose, we will want it to be dynamic, that is to say that we will want it to grow and shrink with the number of entries in the container class, instead of being a single, fixed size.

In this case, for C++ and Turbo Pascal with Objects a dynamic array will work the best, and for Smalltalk we will use an OrderedCollection.

We will be storing a list of orders within a customer, and also, as we look at our analysis, within the business. The business stores its own orders for Items, of course, but it also keeps track of all of its customers' orders. We notice that we will be duplicating data, and quite a bit of it for that matter, with this particular scheme. We can decide during this phase that it might be appropriate for us to store the actual Orders in one class, and keep something unique by which to identify the orders in the other class.

As we look at our Order class, a subclass of Transaction, we notice that we have no unique data member in either class. We did not feel it was necessary at the time, but now it may be. We need to decide whether the savings of storage and memory outweigh the disadvantage of adding a data member that we obviously did not feel was necessary during the analysis.

When making these kinds of decisions, it is often helpful to look at a scenario that might occur during run-time. Suppose that we have many customers, who each have several orders. Each order stores a list of payments, which is also duplicated, and a list of items, which is duplicated. Our view begins to get complicated as we look at this quite likely scenario in *Figure 7.2.*

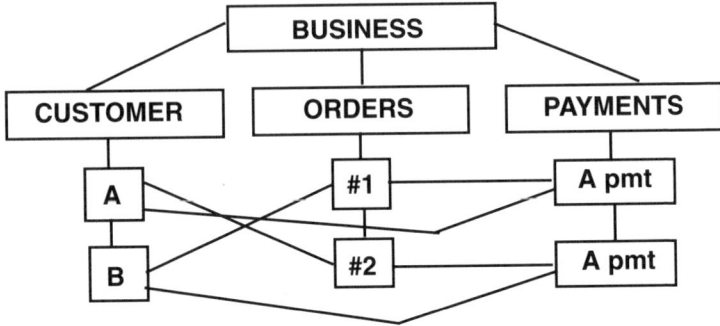

Figure 7.2 : Run-Time Hierarchy.

Obviously, we have created a monster, even with the tiny amount of data we have included. Imagine what this picture would look like with 50 customers, 50 orders and 100 payments. We notice that perhaps storing a list of actual objects may make things much more complex than we had desired. Of course many will say 'But they're just pointers to the same object!' They would be correct. But these objects are persistent, that is, they will be stored somewhere and recreated, reinstantiated, and all of these pointers must not only be represented somehow within the storage medium, but also the pointers must be hooked up when the objects are reinstantiated.

So suppose that we left the model as it is, and we will be storing these objects in a database file. We cannot store a pointer in a data member. We could, but to store a pointer means to store a memory address, and that memory address has a scope only as long as the life of the object. When the object is written to disk, that memory address is meaningless, and our data is ostensibly lost. We must therefore use some unique identifier with which to find the data members that are objects later on.

A popular technique is to store file offsets as a type of tangible pointer to another object within a file. While this will work, imagine the maintenance involved in attempting to update the pointers if an object moves within the file. Imagine the file I/O you are creating by using this type of storage. File I/O is slow even on Pentiums. And, if we are going to be storing some unique identifier, why not use it within the application as well?

There are many times that a user will want to access a customer's information without needing to pull up his payments and or orders at the same time. Why pull all of that information into memory if we don't need to? Performance will be increased because the size of our objects is smaller, and storage becomes much simpler a process both to create, recreate and maintain.

Given these factors, we will store both Orders and Payments within the Customer as a list of unique identifiers. Because most companies have some sort of numbering scheme for receipts (which are payments) and invoices (which are technically orders), this should not cause a problem and in fact will help us model the real world more consistently.

So our view of Order and Payment has changed. We now view them as holding a unique identifier. Because these classes are both derived from Transaction, it makes sense to add this unique number to the class Transaction, so that both Orders and Payments may have easy access to it, and so that we are not creating redundant code. Customer will then store as its list of Orders a list of these numbers, and the list of Payments as a list of their unique identifiers. We will consider them to be unsigned integers also. The process we have just gone through holds tightly to the idea of data encapsulation. We should not, from outside the class, need to worry about how the data is stored. Given a unique identifier, we will be able to find an Order or a Payment quickly and efficiently through the business' global list of the objects. When we look at an Order, we see that it, too, stores a list of payments. We take the same view as with Orders and Payments for a Customer, and will store the list of Payments as a list of unique integers.

The last class we need to examine, in regards to data typing, is Item. It needs to know the number in stock, which will be an integer of some sort; the level at which the business should order more of the item, also an integer; the price to the customer and the cost to the business, both floats. This class was relatively simple to decide because it stores no references to other classes.

Now that the data typing for our classes is complete, we need to look at data manipulation more closely. We can assume that all classes will have standard accessor methods, those which will set and get their respective data members from outside the class, but what about actual manipulation methods?

To answer these questions, we now ask the question of each class; what does it do? For example, a Customer places an order and makes payments. From this we know that we will need data methods for **placeOrder** and **paymentMade**. We also dismissed a class earlier called Bill, deciding instead to make it a method within the Customer class. Therefore, we will need a method **createBill**, which will create a bill based on the customer's orders and payments made lists.

We look at an Order, which stores Items, Payments, and a total cost. What does an order do? It calculates the total cost, based on each item in its list of items, to the customer. We'll call it **calculateTotalBalance**, and it can return the balance due on the Order by subtracting the amount of each Payment from the total cost, **calculateBalanceDue**.

Looking at Business becomes more complicated, for its necessary manipulations to the data are more complex than any of the other classes. It should be able to tell the owner the amount due in from customers, and the amount the business is paying out for orders, **dueFromCustomers**, and **owedForOrders**. It should be able to give us a list of Items that the business needs to order and create the orders necessary, **needToOrder** and **createOrders**. It should also be able to print all the customer's bills out in order for them to be sent to the customer, **printCustomerBills**.

These methods are more complex in many ways, and less complex in other ways. The method **dueFromCustomers** must iterate over the list of customers and return to the Business a total amount due from all customers on all orders. We have in Customer a method that can print out a bill, but we need something more general that just gives us the total amount due.

To make this easier, we will add a method **totalBalanceDue** in Customer, and use it within the business method in order to determine this amount of money. While printing the Bills from the Business is simple enough — an iteration over the customer list telling each one to createBill, and voila, we have created the bills.

But from a customer standpoint it is more difficult than that because a customer must create an actual bill by finding each order, finding its corresponding payments, and printing this information out to either a file, a printer, or the screen. As one abstracts higher and higher, the work involved in a process becomes simpler. This is as it should be in the object paradigm.

We have talked a lot about the design for each class, but have not created anything tangible with which we could begin the actual development process (as most programmers see it). We need to create a design document — something that will convey our intentions and assumptions about the class to the developer, and that will allow us to well document our decisions, analysis and design.

There is no right way to design, and there are as many different formats as there are developers. The key is to find the right mixture of detail for your developers and stick with the format. Consistency is the key. If everyone creates his design documents in his own format, you have lost much of what can be gained from design documents, from both a managerial and a developer's point of view. For that reason, engage the designers and developers in the decision, and find a format that works for you and your team. We use a format that we have found effective on several projects, and feel comfortable with presenting to you as we create the design documents for several of the classes we have worked through in this chapter.

Class Person

The Class Person is responsible for storing and manipulating the data associated with a Person.

Data members of this class are:
- name
- ID number
- address
- phone number

114

Class Considerations (Assumptions)

This class will be used as the base for several other classes and was designed with reusability in mind. For that purpose, application specific data and code will not be placed in this class.

Class Description

- default **constructor**, sets all data to zeroes (NULL)
- a **constructor** which takes the name of the customer and sets all other data members to zeroes
- the **destructor** destroys all data members
- standard accessor methods for all data members

In C^{++} we would need to specify what the access attributes of the data members, and methods, would be. Data would most likely be protected, because it will be manipulated by subclasses, and all the methods — because they are simple accessors,— should probably be public methods. There are many legitimate reasons for making methods private, so do not hesitate to make a method private if you determine that it is necessary to keep the manipulation of data inside the class.

Class Customer

This class is responsible for storing information about a customer, as well as recording the orders and payments of a customer. A customer should be easy to access whether by name or by number.

Data members of this class are:
- orders
- payments

Class Considerations

This class is derived from Person, and will access Person's data members through standard accessor methods. The Orders and Payments lists will store unique integers whose value can quickly find the represented Order or Payment in the master list stored in the Business.

Class Description

- default **constructor** sets all data to zeroes.
- **constructor** takes name and sets all other data to zeroes.
- **destructor** destroys the lists and their associated orders and payments in the master list, and then destroys all other data.
- standard accessor methods.
- **placeOrder** creates an order, fills out the information required, adds the order to the master list and adds the order's identification number to the customer's list of orders.
- **paymentMade** creates a payment, fills out required information adds the payment to the master list, adds the payment's identification number to its associated order and the customers' list of payments.
- **totalBalanceDue** iterates over the list of orders. For each order find all it's associated payments and subtract the total from the total balance due on the order. Return the total balance due from all orders.

We could continue to create design documents for each of the classes we have gone through the analysis and design stages for, but we don't like beating a dead horse. We won't go into implementation details, because at this point we still haven't decided which language to use, and it is really quite irrelevant.

We would point out here, however, that when the coding begins, the developer should be aware of the code they are writing from day one. Some believe that it is better to rush through the implementation and get the code working right and then worry about optimization and performance.

We do not believe that you can ignore these facets of development during the design or implementation stages, because they are an integral part of the decision making process during those phases. We made several decisions based on performance, size of the application, and complexity of the model during the design phase. It would be much more difficult to return to this stage once the code is up and running and redesign and recode pieces of the application.

Object-oriented systems tend to be more integrated and dependent upon each individual piece than the traditionally structured pieces. This may seem like a disadvantage, but we receive the advantages of more closely modeling the real world, and receiving for our efforts reusable pieces of code along the way.

Decisions made early can be painful to the project in the last stages of development. Keep this in mind as you begin doing analysis and design, and don't be afraid to throw away prototype code early on if you see problems inherent in the system. In the end, you will have created a better application, with performance and maintenance requirements that are more acceptable to everyone.

CHAPTER 8
Complexity Management

Because object orientation lends itself so well to the creation of complex systems, management is needed to prevent it from overwhelming not only the original developers, but those who must maintain the code in future years. There is a tendency for those who design object-oriented systems to ignore the implications of complexity in systems or overlook them. Some developers new to the paradigm often do not realize the dangerous road that they must travel in the future when building an extremely complex system.

Often, when complexity is an issue, the ease in which object orientation lends itself to solving complex relationships within a real-world model wins out over a more complex solution that may require more work, and may create more complex relationships. Simply, the easiest implementation may not always be the best solution to the problem, especially when looking toward the future.

While object technology gives us the ability to solve larger problems and write more complex systems in a shorter period of time, its aim is not to make the job of the programmer so much easier that there is no challenge to the developer's job. We have heard developers say 'But it would be easier to do it this way' without any concern for the future of the code or the business needs.

This attitude does not lend itself well to the management of complex systems, and makes the job of future modifications to the code much more time consuming and costly.

Advantages of Managing Complexity Efficiently

The advantages of managing complexity may seem trivial at the onset of a project. Yet even object-oriented systems must store its data *somewhere*, and more often than not it is in some sort of file system, whether that be a database or elaborate system of flat files. Even object databases, heralding their wares, screaming about persistence, must eventually rely on file based storage, which means limits on space and concern over access times.

Imagine a system such as the one in *Figure 8.1 (pg.123)*. Consider how it would be stored on disk. Class A stores a reference to Class D which stores a reference to Class A, etc. But on disk, you cannot simply store pointers or references to other classes. You may consider storing file offsets to instances of each class contained within another, but when reinstantiating these objects how do you know where to stop? How many levels deep do you read before you consider the class to be complete?

You may decide to store some sort of marker that indicates that the application can stop reading in the objects, and this will most certainly work, but consider the nature of the beast you have just created. You must now store more information than just what is stored in the classes just to insure that it is stored correctly. And imagine writing these objects back to the disk. What if they grow in size?

The complexity of the file itself would overwhelm most developers and certainly be prone to corruption and difficulties in debugging while developing the system. It would be more complex than the system itself.

Some may counter by replying that the database system with which they are interfacing and using to store their data handles all that for them and therefore they don't need to worry about such trivial things. However, you still need to be concerned about the size of the system because that is the only factor in this file system you can control.

Certainly you can see that the more nested references stored the more space it takes to store them, and the longer it will take to reinstantiate any single object, regardless how elaborate the database system underlying the storage facility. When an entire department is relying on a database's information every minute, it is a scary thing to have your database system crash because you have run out of disk space. Not every company can simply run out and purchase more hardware every time the file system outgrows its current boundaries.

Most developers are aware that I/O is the bottleneck of any system, small or large. Solving your space needs by continually adding more storage space for months and months, and logically linking them, to form one logical drive, your system's performance is going to drop like a heavy rock from the top of the Empire State Building. By avoiding back references and deeply nested objects, you can avoid extremely nasty performance times and storage problems, making the users of your system happier and thus more productive, and making the developer's job that much more rewarding.

In addition to the pitfalls possible in a system that is extremely complex, there are the pitfalls that eventually drive developers to the padded room in the nearest mental health facility. Imagine perusing through code with deeply nested objects, or reading documents which reference each other which reference each other which reference each other, in an attempt to learn the system so that you can make a simple change to the code.

If you were not involved in the implementation or design of the system, it may take days instead of hours to make what ought to be a simple change to the system. Software developers who are new to the code can become confused and lost inside code that is more complex than it had to be, had the maintenance of the system been considered when the design was done in the first place.

Even those who implemented or had a hand in the design of a system could become confused if they are away from the system for a time. These factors must be considered early, and continue to be a part of the implementation of any system in order to insure that the program will have a long life and live up to the expectations of the paradigm (and your users!).

Decisions About Data

Perhaps the easiest way to prevent complexity from taking over your system is to carefully consider how you are storing your data within an object. It is very easy and tempting to allow Class A to hold a pointer to Class B, and later allow Class B to hold a pointer to Class A, but consider the problem growing larger and larger, until your system is overrun with back references from deeply nested objects within a class back to the original class *(Figure 8.1)*.

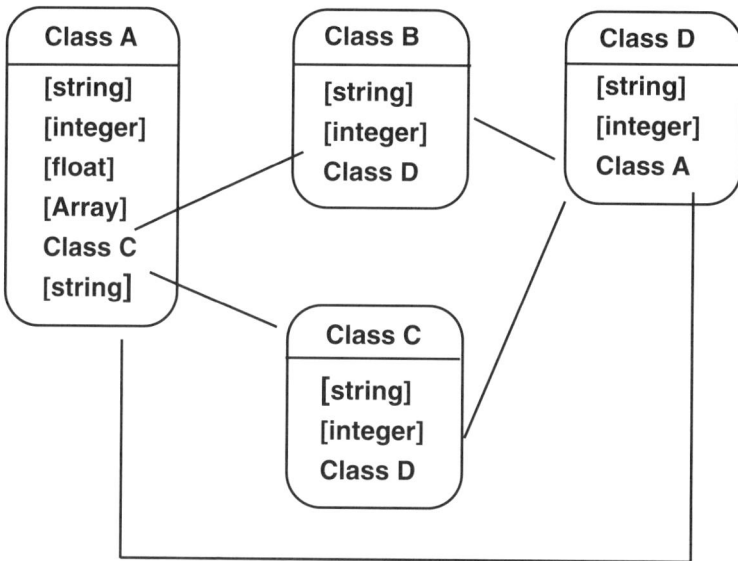

Figure 8.1: Back Referencing Classes.

Suppose in Class A the integer is a unique identifier of the object. In any given application, there will never be two instances of Class A with this instance variable the same. Suppose also that Class D requires for its operation a reference to Class A. With these requirements, the easiest solution is as pictured in *Figure 8.1*. Simply give Class D a pointer to an actual instance of Class A.

However, in a very large system, this back referencing will begin to have problems. Debugging becomes a hideous process, and provability is thrown out of the window. Because every instance of Class A is uniquely identified by its integer instance variable, it would be a better solution to store in Class D only the integer instance variable of the instance of Class A instead of, ostensibly, class A itself.

You may cringe in horror — 'But that's not true object orientation!' In a pure language it is, because an integer is an object in such a system. A method added to the integer class called asClassA ,which finds the correct instance of class A based on the integer. In other impure languages, it still is given that the important part of an object system is not that everything is an object. We should not care how the data is stored within an object. Whether the data is a unique integer that can represent an instance of Class A, or whether the data is actually a pointer to Class A *should be irrelevant*. As long as we are given an accessor that can return to us the instance of Class A which Class D is referencing the method of storage is completely irrelevant.

Given this fact, it is best to consider complexity when making decisions about the representation of objects in a model. This option has some advantages:

- Class D does not have the burden of storing a class which ultimately stores itself which stores a class which ultimately stores itself, and so on.

124

- Speed of execution increases since the system is much more compact without the referential relationships which can also cause moving within memory to become dangerous.

- Uses less memory and I/O storage because of the decrease in the size of the objects.

- Documentation of the system is much clearer making it easier to bring in new developers to maintain existing code and implement new features.

- Debugging is much simpler.

Decisions About Class Hierarchies

Another simple way to keep complexity down is to attempt to limit the number of classes that will have to be changed in the future. In short, generalize as much as possible.

A debit and a credit are both transactions, and both hold a dollar amount, a date, an identification code of some sort, and (usually) a breakdown of where the money went or came from. So make sure to sweep your system frequently looking for similarities in classes that could be placed in superclasses or subclasses. We've seen cases where every subclass of a given class implement the same exact code. That not only adds complexity, it destroys object orientation, and wastes time because you have to modify the code in several different places, instead of just one.

Complexity management is growing as object technology emerges into the business world as a mainstream method of programming. It is as necessary as the analysis and design phases, and should be carefully considered during the implementation phase of any object-oriented system. As the field of complexity management emerges, make it a point to familiarize yourself with the ideas and concepts being researched.

Keep It Simple

Avoid deeply nested objects. Objects nested one or even two deep are not a major danger to a system, except when they become back referencing. By back referencing, we mean the situation that occurred in *Figure 8.1*, with a class nested three levels deep referencing the initial node in the hierarchy. Usually, there is at least one unique data member in any class, and this is usually a good place to start when looking to remove nested objects from your system.

Ignore the cries from absolute purists about the destruction of the paradigm — they are quite simply not living in the real world— and go ahead and use those unique data members to remove nested references. If there is not a unique data member to use, try more tried and true methods. Most database systems have record numbering schemes or unique identifiers that you can access. Your system has to resolve these problems, so use it to solve your complexity problems before they begin. If you aren't using a database system, and are instead using a flat file system, try using file offsets. They are always unique, and can be used to a deficit of only the size of a long integer: 8 bytes. Not bad considering the alternative.

Design before you implement. Too many developers want to jump into code. Too often we are knee deep in code before we realize that the system is going to be too complex, and by that time we don't want to throw away the code and start again. So we continue on, throwing in references here and there and creating a monster.

To solve this problem, design before you begin to code. A design document is much easier to throw away and start again than is actual code. This method, of course, does not go hand-in-hand very well with the spiral, or iterative, method of software development. Designing pieces at a time, coding them, and then recoding them, lends itself to exactly the opposite of what we are trying to accomplish — less complex systems.

The waterfall method works wonders for diminishing instances of complex systems, because the entire system is laid out before real code is written. With this method, you can make changes to design here and there where it is needed in order to compensate for complexity. As developers, we hate to throw away code after it is written, and by designing first and coding later, we reduce the chances of having to throw away code, and also make the system less complex and more efficient at the same time.

Documentation is NOT just for management. Documentation can be one of the most important pieces of your system longevity. Documentation can make it easier for new developers to learn the system, and makes maintenance and upgrading an easy task. Documentation also provides a chance for the developer to explain code or decisions made about the implementation, as well as truly understand the code he or she has written. It will make other developers more at ease in code that they have not written, and if the documentation includes the name or initials of the developer who wrote the code, gives others someone to go to if the code is not understood or advice on improvements is required.

Documentation can be beneficial both to the developers implementing the system, and to those who will maintain and upgrade the system. It reduces complexity not by changing the code, but by allowing for a little extra explanation about the system without having to rely upon the implementor's presence.

Use a run-time hierarchy to prove correctness. Most people don't understand what we mean by this, because you do it every day in structured programming, and never put a name to it. You know that at run-time, your Customer Record has a Person record as a piece of it. That's a run-time hierarchy. Unlike our is_a notation, this is simply a diagram of run-time ownership.

If you cannot draw a diagram of who owns what at run-time, you are building too complex a system. An example of your Class Hierarchy is shown in *Figure 8.2.*

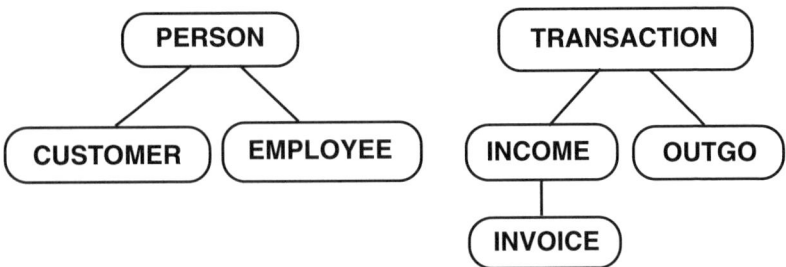

8.2 : A Partial Class Hierarchy.

128

Each of your customers will have a series of purchases (you hope!), and the best place to store them would be under Customer, in some kind of collection. Then each Customer would have his own list of invoices. Your run-time hierarchy would then look like *Figure 8.3*.

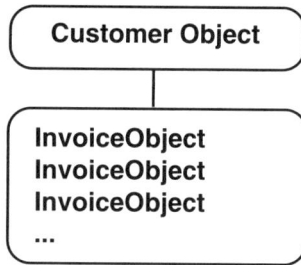

```
 _____
|                                |
|        Customer Object         |
|_____|
                |
 _____|_____
|                                |
|   InvoiceObject                |
|   InvoiceObject                |
|   InvoiceObject                |
|   ...                          |
|_____|
```

Figure 8.3 : Run-Time Hierarchy.

Simple, and to-the-point. One of the pitfalls we talked about would be to assume that each invoice knew who its Customer was. That could be found through the list of all customers, and saves you a reference to Customer in each invoice.

Imagine *Figure 8.3*, with lines back from each Invoice up to its customer. This is a rather simple case you can avoid. We have seen much worse.

Sometimes, it is necessary to place a reference to an object that refers to this one. We are saying you should avoid it as much as possible. A global list of all instances of an object is one way to do that, giving the list the ability to find instances rapidly. Then, your data isn't self-referential (in a round about way), but you can still get at what you need.

Optimizations

The world is full of purists. We know, we're two of them. If you're going to make the move to OO, do it, and don't go half-way. We've seen many cases where a lack of adherence to object-oriented strictures caused serious problems.

There comes a time (optimization time, usually), when you must leave the path of the purist, and delve into reality. Object-oriented languages are slower and produce larger binary (executable) files than their procedural counterparts. Anyone who attempts to tell you different is sadly misinformed.

In most cases, the speed of our machines makes that difference negligible, and the increased efficiency of each programmer on a team makes up for much of that loss in execution speed. But, when the time comes to deliver, and your application shows signs of unacceptable performance, it is time to consider optimizations. Some of the best optimizations you can make involve structured programming.

In all three of the languages we've used, there is a way to provide an interface into lower-level languages. In C++ and Turbo Pascal with Objects, the use of structured techniques is so dangerously close that we actually read 'Remember, if you don't know how to do it in C++, you can always revert to C...' once. Many books we've read on the subject do suggest using structures if the class you are declaring contains only public members and methods. In Smalltalk, you can call Windows or OS/2 DLL's through the DynamicLinkLibrary class.

In all cases, judiciously choosing things that are screamingly inefficient in the language of choice, and implementing them in a lower level language can improve performance dramatically. Remember though, to wrap your lower level code in an OO 'wrapper' so that the majority of your source code is pure.

The typical example is the one below. While in C and C++ you can access the video memory directly, it is considerably slower than assembly language. Using the asm{} keyword built into most PC C++ assemblers, you could create the following class definition (note that this is an incomplete class, we chose not to reproduce it accurately due to space limitations):

```
class Screen{
    unsigned VidSeg;              // Segment of the video board.
    unsigned CurrOffset;          // Offset into that segment.
    char     ForeGround;          // ForeGround Color.
    char     BackGround;          // BackGround Color.
Public:
    Screen(unsigned videoSeg = 0xB800){ VidSeg = videoSeg;
        CurrOffset=0;}
    ~Screen(){}
    //Accessors
    unsigned currOffset(){return CurrOffset;}
    void currOffset(unsigned newOffset;){currOffset = newOffset;}
    char foreGround(){return ForeGround;}
    char backGround(){return BackGround;}
    void foreGround(char newColor){ForeGround = newColor;}
    void backGround(char newColor){BackGround = newColor << 4;}
    // Extended Accessors
    char colorByte(){return ForeGround | BackGround;}
    char far *currVideoPointer(){return ((((long) VidSeg )<< 16) |
        CurrOffset);}

    // Character output methods
    putChar(char what, int row=0, int col=0);
    ...
```

```
};
Screen::putChar(charwhat,introw=0, intcol=0)
{
    unsignedtempColor = colorByte;
    if(row > 0 || col > 0)
        CurrOffset = (row - 1) * 80 + (col - 1)*2;
    asm{
                        mov    di,CurrOffset
                        mov    es,VidSeg
                        mov    ah, tempColor
                        mov    al,what
                        mov    [es:di],ax        ;mov char+attr to location
    }
    return;
}
```

You have a much faster (and useful in real life) implementation than one that relies on **cout** but which is still object-oriented to the caller of the Screen class. There are many simpler ways to handle optimization, but each project is different, and you'll have to find out how much speed you need to gain, and how much time you have to complete the optimization. Assembly language (any lower level language for that matter) is, by its very nature, harder to write, debug, and maintain than an object-oriented language, so this technique should only be followed when speed is of the essence, and you use the class in question often.

CHAPTER 9
People Problems

It has been said that the only thing that remains a constant in our world is change. Change, for many people, can be an intimidating thing. A radical shift in paradigms is a big change, one that may cause fear and resentment among the developers who are being asked to change. Organizational change, when not handled properly, can cause a decrease in productivity, morale, and of course, profits. Change must be introduced in such a way that make the developer feel as comfortable as possible, making it clear that they, as well as the company, will benefit from the change.

We do not pretend to be experts in the area of organizational communication, and so we will not try to tell you how to go about instituting a change from a structured arena to an object-oriented paradigm. We will, however, give you some insight into the effects of such a shift in paradigms as we have viewed them in organizations.

The Effects of the Switch

Moving from a structured environment to an object-oriented environment involves much more than just the paradigm swing. Because object orientation is so much more than just a programming technique, it can be difficult to move developers from one to the other easily and without hassle. Analysis and design methodologies must be changed, coding styles must often change, and the relationships between the developers, analysts, and users often take radical shifts in order to successfully move from one arena to another.

A new methodology is not only a change in technique, but a change in the relationship between the analysts. No longer can a manager dole out responsibility for analysis of a single piece of the puzzle to individuals. Indeed, all analysts of a single application must work together during the analysis phase in order to remove complex problems in later stages of development.

Without Class A knowing how to talk to Class B and other such sticky issues, a project simply cannot come together. Analysts, while perhaps responsible for only a few classes each in a development effort, must work in a cohesive unit in order to insure that protocols are common across the application, and to insure that the methods in which information is passed between classes will be appropriate.

Adaptation to message protocol is still a necessity, but it is much easier to add a simple method to a class than it is to add a new function to a module, especially when the information being derived from that particular method may seem to be ancillary to most developers.

First things first. If you are one of the people making the switch, you must be professional enough to acknowledge that, no matter how much knowledge and prestige you had as a structured programmer, you are entering a paradigm in which you know nothing. You will flounder and probably give up if you cannot accept that you don't know it all already. When you truly begin to learn the object-oriented paradigm, all of your experience will be a huge asset, but until you leave that experience (and your ego), on the shelf for a few months, you will not learn the object-oriented paradigm.

We've seen people with years of structured programming become excellent object-oriented developers, but the ones that make it are those that can realize how different even the train of thought must be, for object technology to work correctly for your department.

The Management Factor

If you are a manager of developers moving to the object world, then tread warily. No one likes to lose the people that have built and maintained their legacy systems, but there are inevitably one or two people who, even in the face of the overwhelming evidence available that says object orientation is here to stay, will fight tooth and nail to avoid making the transition.

If you cannot find a way to motivate these people, it is our suggestion that you let them go with the system they are hanging on to. That's a very cold view, but your company is in business to make money, and if you are making an honest effort to move your people from one platform to another and there's an employee who won't take it upon himself to try, then your conscience should be clear, and your department better off.

Perhaps those who are not willing to make the transition from programming one language to another can be persuaded to learn in order to be analysts for the company. Their business knowledge is important to your development staff, and if they can learn at least the rudimentary skills necessary to keep up with more experienced developers in the object realm, their input on the business process side of things may well benefit the company.

As we've said already, don't hold on to them if they won't budge on the subject, or if they make things worse instead of better. Business' should not be charity centers. Holding on to those who will not move with the company take up the space that could be used for those who will move and will benefit the company even more.

Managers should also be wary when hiring. Demand proof, and check references, not just that they were where they said, but that they were doing what they claimed. We have seen some truth stretching that is bordering on unbelievable, as more and more people try to get experience in the paradigm.

If you are looking for experienced developers, come up with a test, or a short quiz. We saved quite a bit of time using a short, six question quiz when interviewing C++ developers. Make the questions hard enough to throw people who are stretching the truth, but not so hard that no one can answer them. We don't like to doubt everyone, but when you are making a resource decision for your employer, better to be safe than sorry.

Last, but not least, a manager should not be afraid to use the 90-day probation built into most employment offers to dump someone who snuck past your interview process. While this is not a good clause to invoke often, if the person doesn't fit your needs, don't shackle yourself with them.

We've seen several cases where an employee clearly didn't fit the qualifications required, and they were kept beyond the probationary period. Doing so does nothing for you, your company, or the employee. In the end, they are either buried with work they cannot perform, or (more often), shuffled off to do work on legacy systems. This is probably not the solution either the employee, or employer were looking for, and instead of swinging momentum toward the paradigm shift occurring, you have just tipped the scales back to the structured realm.

Promote Team Spirit

Software development today is a team effort. You cannot get away from the fact that with the size and complexity of the requests we get, the project is usually beyond the ability of one or two people to implement in a reasonable amount of time. With teams, there must come team spirit in order for your project to be the best it can.

Strangely enough, people think of different things when they hear team spirit. We do not mean department spirit, or devotion to the company, we mean developers having a firm belief that their team is the best, and their product will be a better product than any other in the department. You might view this as dividing your department, but isn't that what teams are all about? The work has been divided between different teams, so why not the loyalty? Developers who believe they are working on something special will do a better job, and are easier to hold accountable for their actions by the rest of the team.

By the same token, blame should never be placed to anyone outside of your team. To the outside world, you are working on a project, and if it is not done on time, the team failed. That is the face you should present to the whole company, to provide developers with some leeway for mistakes. To someone from another department, such as marketing or sales, a developer could say 'Sorry, we blew it.', but when alone, could ask the person who kept the project from deadline completion what went wrong.

If you are a team leader, remember that if this project doesn't come in on time, you will shoulder most of the blame. That is the way it should be, because you are responsible for the overall project. It is the team leader's responsibility to delegate responsibility throughout the team, to insure that each member is meeting their individual deadlines, and to facilitate communication between team members. You are the only one who truly knows exactly what is going on at any given point in the project.

Promotions Without Problems

More than any other paradigm, OO lets the best float to the top. In order to be a good developer, you have to know the paradigm well. If you know the paradigm well, then you're a prime candidate for OOA/OOD. But to be a good analyst, you must work well with people (your customers), so that means you'd probably (though definitely not always) be a good project leader. Don't hesitate to move people up the scale, but be aware of one thing: Good developers, when pushed too far too fast from the development arena, will move on to somewhere that they can be good developers again.

Both of us have left jobs where, in less than a year, we were given leadership of projects on such a large scale that we feared for our technical ability, being overwhelmed with managerial responsibilities and project management duties. Both of us are now employed at different companies, and the employer in question in at least one case, has made the same error of judgment again, and lost a third developer.

The moral of the story is: Let your people decide their rate of advancement, and compensate them accordingly. Do not punish those who feel it is not time for them to move up yet. If you resent them for their decision, they may very well go elsewhere to a company where their decisions about their career will be better received, and given more respect. People know what they want, and how fast they want it, so give them some say in the matter, no matter how urgent your needs seem.

Code and Design Reviews

Quite often, software developers see design and code reviews as an attempt to look over their shoulder. It is a manager's job to present these necessary tools in a light that will be acceptable to your developers. While design reviews help developers and users insure that they are on the same page, the real benefit of code reviews is not an immediate improvement in the quality of the software being written, but rather a long-term improvement in several other areas.

Design reviews can often help if business processes or user requirements are in question. If the analysis is done well, a non-developer should be able to read the document and relate it to his requirements, with little or no help from a developer. That being the case, take the design back to the people who know what the system should do, the users if possible, or the user requirement writers. A design review can expand interdepartmental communication, and reaffirm the desire of the developers to produce a product that is clearly what the user wants. It is a time for the developer to insure that he is fulfilling the requirements, and a time for the requirements people and/or users to calm their anxieties about a project in someone else's hands.

A simple design review might consist of the following:

- *The Team Leader: You need the team leader to make decisions about what can be changed if large changes are requested, and to insure that the communication between departments is being handled well.*

- *The Designer: The developer who wrote the design document needs to be there! He is the one who knows what is meant by what is written, and may need to have questions of his own answered.*

- *The Users/Requirements Writers: These people are very important to the meeting as they will determine whether the design fulfills the requirements.*

- *Another Developer: This seemingly ancillary person puts the designer at ease by having "one of their own" present, and fulfills the role of determining implementation validity of the design.*

Have the designer walk through the design, explaining what it is they are writing, and how it fulfills the requirements. Have the developer ask questions if something seems like it might not be possible, implementation wise, and validate the design for implementation. Allow questions and answers between all members of the meeting, as it enhances communication and relationships between departments, and insures that needs are being met.

Code reviews improve many portions of the software development process, and stimulate your developers' imagination. The most significant improvement caused by code reviews usually comes in the form of standardization of styles.

When someone does something very differently than the rest of your team, peer pressure will pull him into the mainstream, making maintenance easier. It also improves the dissemination of information, as people have a chance at the code review, to ask questions they normally would attempt to puzzle through on their own.

The code review is a prime place for technical wizards to introduce new techniques and ideas. If code reviews are conducted at the team level, it also helps to stimulate team spirit and camaraderie, by allowing the team some time together without their faces buried in monitors.

A code review team should be as different from a design review team as the job of coding is different from the job of designing. The primary purpose of code reviews should be to give everyone on the team a familiarity with what the other members are doing, while the primary goal of a design review is to prove to the users (or requirements writers, if your software is for outside sales) that their needs are being met, and prove to the developers that you are not giving them a design that's practically impossible to implement. Our experience has shown that the following is an acceptable code review team:

- *The Team Leader: It is the team leader's responsibility to insure that the pieces will mesh to make a coherent whole. He should preside over the review, keeping the comments constructive and also keep an eye on how this piece relates to the whole of the project.*

- *Two to Four Team Members: We did our best to arrange code reviews so that most people present had code to be reviewed. The number should be enough to make the programmer presenting his code feel like there are more developers present than other people. These people should be watching for code quality and adherence to department coding standards.*

- *The Designers of the Code to be Reviewed: In order to keep the number of people who are not performing their primary job function to a minimum, we had designers come to the review only for review of the implementation of their particular designs. It is their task to insure that the code fulfills the design.*

Testing is Part of the Development Life Cycle

In far too many departments across the country today, testing is treated as a secondary job by software developers. Testing is perhaps one of the most important stages of the software development process, as it insures the quality of the design and implementation. Testing finds programming errors, as well as logical flaws in the design. It is an integral part of the process and should not be left to last minute checks and 'if we have time'attitudes. If your users are doing your testing, they won't be back for the next version.

There are several applications on the market that can aid in the testing effort. Microsoft's MSTest allows code to be written that will automate the testing process, and give your code a thorough walk through. By removing the manual click here, enter data there, testing becomes less of a chore to developers and leaves more time for fixing the errors found by the testing application.

Be wary though, automated testing software won't catch all of your errors. There still needs to be an employee who is thoroughly dedicated to the quality of the software developers are writing, and will walk through the application checking for cosmetic errors, subtle logical errors, and the general look and feel of the application. For C++, Nu-Mega's BoundsChecker (for DOS or Windows) will catch all those subtle memory errors that aren't caught or aren't easily reproduced, and can aid in finding out exactly what is causing major blow ups that can't be found through debuggers.

Testers should be involved throughout the development process, learning the application, what the users expect, and how the application should react. Writing test suites, which cover from every menu item to every help screen, can be a big aid to insuring software quality. As each piece of code is completed, the tester can run the completed portions of code through the appropriate test suite and declare it worthy of being released, or send it back to the development staff with detailed explanations of what went wrong when and where.

This is particularly important in an object-oriented system where developers are implementing classes separately that must interact with each other. As our systems grow more complex, the need for quality assurance grows exponentially. Adding testing to the software development process at each step insures that the quality of the application which will be released to your users, will be of the highest quality. Inevitably, a developer will code a class which, on its own, performs flawlessly, but when combined with other classes in the system will either itself work incorrectly, or cause other classes to perform incorrectly.

The job of the tester is to find these errors, the causes, and return to the developer with information that will help them in correcting the errors and raising the quality of the code. While a tester need not be a programmer, a tester should have a thorough knowledge of the tool he is using for testing purposes, the application they are testing, and the requirements of the application. A working knowledge of the operating system(s) the application will be running under, and an understanding of the software development process is a definite plus.

Give your tester(s) the credit they deserve. They are a part of your team and deserve to be treated as your friend, and not your enemy. After all, the tester(s) are working towards the same goal the developers are — quality object-oriented software that meets the needs of the users.

Glossary

ADT (abstract data type). A basic data type in programming, this refers most often to lists, queues, stacks and other container type data types.

Abstract. Class that contains one or more virtual methods and cannot be instantiated.

Abstraction (data). Grouping related pieces of data together into logical units, usually modeled after the business processes that a system must interact with.

Analysis. Process of determining the major components of a model and their interaction in the real-world; "what we have to do."

Attributes. The data associated with a class.

Base class. A class from which any other class is derived; used to group shared behaviors and data in one place.

Class. The definition of an object, includes data and methods that manipulate the data. A logical grouping of data.

Constructor. Special method which creates an instance of a class.

Data member. A piece of data stored within a class or instance.

Derived. A class that inherits from (is a subclass of) another class is said to be derived from the other class.

Design. Process of specifying objects that correspond to the real-world entity that you are attempting to model, giving those objects names, attributes and methods.

Destructor. Special method that destroys an instance of a class; not needed in Smalltalk because of its advanced memory management.

Dynamic. Memory allocated at run-time.

Encapsulation (data). Data hiding, 'need-to-know' basis of allowing data to be visible or not; process that makes knowing the data type of data members irrelevant; specifics of implementation are hidden from all of the system except for this class.

GUI (graphical user interface). Most common term for the interface of applications written for Microsoft Windows, X Windows, and other such window based systems.

Hierarchy. Like a lineage, shows the relationships between objects either at run-time or as an inheritance tree.

Inheritance. The process of subclassing, children receive data and methods from their parents.

Instance (object). The product of class instantiation, an instance of a class. This is the actual entity through which messages are passed, data is manipulated, and the application is run .

Instantiation. The process of calling a class' constructor, thereby creating an instance of that class.

Message. The call made to a member function or method, you may not know the type of class you are sending the message to. — *see polymorphism*.

Method, member function. A member function or operation that manipulates a class' or instance's data members.

Model. Set of classes that emulate real world entities.

Modeling. The process in which you create a model of some real-world entity through analysis and design, in an object-oriented paradigm.

Object orientation. The process of thinking of real-world entities in terms of objects, then implementing those objects in such a way as to create a system that models the real world accurately.

OOA/D. Object-Oriented Analysis and Design.

Overload(ed). Relates to operators in C++, the process of redefining the standard operators (-,+,=, ==) to act upon user defined classes.

Over-ridden (over-ride). Process of redefining a base class' method in a subclass in order to provide more specific behavior.

Persistent (persistence). An object retains its current state no matter what happens to the application.

Protocol. Common naming of methods across a group of classes.

Polymorphism. Different entities respond differently to the same message.

Purely virtual method. Methods contained in a base class that must be over-ridden in subclasses, method of enforcing a common protocol among classes.

Responsibilities. Data manipulation methods for a class.

Spiral. Development process that walks through the analysis-design-code-test phases in small pieces, iterating over the entire process many times throughout the development life cycle.

Static. Memory allocated at compile time (not used in Smalltalk).

Subclass. The child of another class; a class which gets some of its data and methods from another class (called its parent).

Subclassing. The act of creating a subclass.

Typecasting. Processing of making a pointer point to some other type of class, usually done to abstract data from lists that store several types of objects, all whose class is derived from a common base class; not necessary in Smalltalk.

Vacuous. Class that has no data members, any methods in the class definition are purely virtual.

Virtual. A method which, when used in conjunction with inheritance, provides for a common protocol across children of a base class that implement the virtual method.

Waterfall. Development process concept that follows the following steps: analysis, design, code and test, with each step being as complete as possible before moving on to the next.

Bibliography

Eckel, Bruce. *C++ Inside & Out*. Berkley, CA: McGraw-Hill, 1993.

Entsminger, Gary. *The Tao of Objects*. New York, NY: M&T Books, 1990.

Hofstadter, Douglas. *Godel, Escher, and Bach: An Eternal Golden Braid*. New York, NY: Random House, Inc., 1989.

Index

P

S

T

V

W

Also Available from CBM Books

TITLE	PRICE	ISBN
A Practical Guide to Windows NT by Kenneth L. Spencer	$25	1-878956-39-6
The AS/400 Companion by Enck and Ryan	$19	1-878956-45-0
C++: An Introduction for Experienced C Programmers by Rex Jaeschke	$30	1-878956-27-2
Client/Server Programming in PC LANs (disk included) by Barfield and Walters	$45	1-878956-44-2
Data Communications & Networking Dictionary by T.D. Pardoe and R.P. Wenig	$12	1-878956-06-X
Ethernet Tips and Techniques: For Designing , Installing and Troubleshooting Your Ethernet Network by Byron Spinney	$15	1-878956-43-4
Focus On OpenView: A Guide to Hewlett-Packard's Network and Systems Management Platform by Nathan Muller	$40	1-878956-48-5
ISPF/REXX Development for Experienced Programmers (disk included) by Lou Marco	$35	1-878956-50-7
Multimedia Exploration: Working With Tools, Tips, Products and Sources (CD-ROM included) by Jamie Showrank	$39	1-878956-42-6
Navigating The AS/400: A Hands-On Guide by John Enck and Michael Ryan	$39	1-878956-31-0
Network Your Mac (and live to tell about it!): The REAL Beginner's Guide by Carl Powell III	$19	1-878956-41-8
Object-Oriented Programming: A New Way of Thinking by Donald W. and Lori A. MacVittie	$22	1-878956-52-3
OpenVMS Performance Management by James W. Coburn	$40	1-878956-40-X
PATHWORKS V5 Network Administration Guide by Ed Barfield	$39	1-878956-49-3
The Dictionary of Standard C by Rex Jaeschke	$12	1-878956-07-8
Total SNMP: Exploring the Simple Network Management Protocol by Sean Harnedy	$45	1-878956-33-7
TP Software Development for OpenVMS by John M.Willis	$35	1-878956-34-5

To order through your local bookstore just mention the ISBN, or order direct from CBM Books by calling TOLL FREE 1-800-285-1755, or fax 215-643-8099. Outside of the U.S. call (215) 643-8105. Prices subject to change.